Getting Started

as an Independent

Computer Consultant

Getting Started as an Independent Computer Consultant

An Insider's Guide to Starting, Promoting and
Managing Your Own Successful Consulting Business

Mitch Paioff

Consulting Training Institute

Getting Started as an Independent Computer Consultant
An Insider's Guide to Starting, Promoting and
Managing Your Own Successful Consulting Business

Consulting Training Institute
Littleton, Colorado

Orders: www.cti-seminars.com; info@cti-seminars.com

Unattributed quotations are by Mitch Paioff.

Copyright © 2009 by Mitch Paioff

First Edition

ISBN 978-0-98192-970-5

Book Design by www.KarrieRoss.com

Printed in Canada

Library of Congress Control Number: 2008940807

. . .

Table of Contents

About the Author

Mitch Paioff has been a successful independent computer consultant for many years. He is the author of several books including *Accounting Software Guide* and *50 New Tax Clients a Year*.

Mitch spends much of his time mentoring technology professionals who are planning to start their own consulting businesses. He has developed a unique coaching methodology that shows new consultants how to be successful in this ever-changing field.

As the author of *Getting Started as an Independent Computer Consultant*, Mitch will share his many insider secrets with his readers. He is considered the leading expert in the independent computer consulting industry.

Mitch was prompted to write this book because so many independent computer consultants wanted to know his secrets to being successful. Now Mitch is revealing them to you—the good life of independent computer consulting.

Acknowledgements

This book would not have been possible without the dedication, patience, and expertise of the following individuals: Dr. Judith Briles, my book shepherd, who has guided me through the book publishing process from the very beginning (www.coloradobookshepherd.com); Melanie Mulhall, the wordsmith who took my rough ideas and magically transformed them into flowing sentences, paragraphs, and chapters (www.thatcopywriter.com); and Karrie Ross, whose creative talents turned a plain book cover and manuscript into works of art (www.karrieross.com).

Of course, there would never have been a book at all if I had not become an independent computer consultant. I want to thank the many great clients with whom I have worked. I also want to thank the small number of clients who contributed to the "Dealing with Difficult Clients" chapter. I have learned much from both groups!

Most of all, I would like to thank my loving wife, Toby, and my handsome son, Joshua, for allowing me to lock myself away in my room for days on end while I worked on what I consider to be an industry-changing guide to starting a computer consulting business.

Warning and Disclaimer

This book is designed to provide information on starting, promoting, and managing a computer consulting business. It is sold with the understanding that the publisher and author are not engaged in rendering legal, accounting, or other professional services. If legal or other expert assistance is required, the services of a competent professional should be sought.

It is not the purpose of this book to restate all the information that is otherwise available to computer consultants but, instead, to complement, amplify, and supplement other texts. You are urged to read all the available material, learn as much as possible about the computer consulting industry, and tailor the information to your individual needs.

Computer consulting is not a get-rich-quick scheme. Anyone who decides to become an independent computer consultant must expect to invest a great deal of time and effort into it. For many people, self-employment is more lucrative than working for a consulting firm, and many independent computer consultants have built solid, growing, rewarding businesses.

Every effort has been made to make this book as complete and accurate as possible. However, there may be mistakes, both typographical and in content. Therefore, this text should be used only as a general guide and not the ultimate source for starting a computer consulting business. Furthermore, this book contains information on computer consulting that is current only up to the printing date.

The purpose of this book is to educate and entertain. The author and Consulting Training Institute shall have neither liability nor responsibility to any person or entity with respect to any loss or damage caused, or alleged to have been caused, directly or indirectly, by the information contained in this book.

If you do not wish to be bound by the above, you may return this book to the publisher for a full refund.

Foreword

I was thrilled when Mitch Paioff asked me to introduce his new book, *Getting Started as an Independent Computer Consultant*. As the Executive Director of the Independent Computer Consultants Association (ICCA), I know that many computer experts have found self-employment to be a terrific way to gain more control over their schedules and to achieve financial success.

There are many books that address the needs of consultants, in general. Mitch Paioff's book is different because he addresses the unique needs of computer consultants. His chapters on marketing and identifying niches are extremely valuable. But by far the most important chapter in his book deals with common mistakes made by new consultants. Despite his success as an independent consultant, Mitch Paioff has obviously made many mistakes in his career. He is not ashamed to admit them publicly and show others how to avoid them.

If you are a computer expert and you are thinking about starting your own business as a consultant, I would highly recommend that you read this book from cover to cover.

Then you should join the ICCA. Mitch made a special request of me to share a bit of information about the ICCA. He truly believes in the organization and feels belonging to ICCA can make all the difference in the world in becoming a successful computer consultant.

Established in 1976, the Independent Computer Consultants Association is a professional community of business information technology computer consultants. ICCA members are the experts clients rely on for independent, unbiased, and ethical consulting relationships providing business analysis, strategic planning, IT infrastructure support, training, website design, software development, and digital media consulting.

Why have thousands of independent IT consultants belonged to ICCA? Because they realize the difference between success for their company and just getting by is ICCA.

Take Member #1, for example. In 2001, he was laid off after the 9-11 attacks and began rebuilding his own life as an independent computer consultant. Using our online discussion forums, he received advice in marketing, taxes, legal, and many other areas. He used our online contract templates to protect his business from lawsuits and attended many of our conferences to learn more about running his business and taking it to the next level.

Member #2 joined ICCA and used our website and our #1 ranking on Google to link back to his own site—which landed him over $100,000 from leads, referrals, and new clients. His clients loved the fact he was part of an association with a well established code of ethics and a nationwide pool of consultants he could call upon for advice.

Member #3 had a very limited amount of start-up money but joined ICCA hoping to save both time and money. The ICCA Standard Form Consulting Contract, as well as the Subcontractor's Agreement, reduced her attorney fees. ICCA's Logo and Client Brochures reduced her marketing expenses. Being placed on the ICCA website with her own home page exposed her to potential clients. She shopped around and ended up purchasing policies from some of our insurance providers (liability, errors and omissions, health, and disability insurance), which saved her a great deal of money. Membership dues each year pay for themselves in what she saves from these benefits and services. She found that starting her business became a whole lot easier!

Member #4 wanted to learn how to run his business. He knew he had the "techie stuff" under control but he wanted to rub elbows with seasoned consultants and learn from their successes . . . as well as failures. He signed up with ICCA's special interest groups (SIGs), which gave him easy access to a pool of consultants in similar business situations. He now participates in the ICCA monthly webinars and he attends the annual ICCA national conferences, where he meets all the "big boys" as he establishes friends and contacts for years to come.

Member #5 was a college student looking to start his own consulting business. He had the drive and the technical knowledge but fell short on the business side of things. He did not know where to begin. Not only did he have no entrepreneurial experience, he also had very little corporate experience. The ICCA helped him to prepare a roadmap for the process he needed to follow. After joining, he was able to use the discussion boards to talk through this process with consultants who had much more experience than him. From there, he formed relationships that benefited his business. The ICCA was responsive to his needs and did not judge him by his age. In addition, the organization gave him some much needed credibility so that when he approached clients, he was able to appear professional and legitimate.

This is just a small sampling of what ICCA has done for some of its members. ICCA is dedicated to helping independent contractors get noticed by companies worldwide who are looking for talented IT professionals and to providing consultants with all their business needs. No matter what your level of experience or areas of expertise, ICCA can help you learn how to build your company into a successful consulting business.

The difference between success and just getting by for your company is ICCA. Validate your skills, promote your business, and increase your marketing potential. And I might mention, as you might have suspected, Mitch Paioff is a member of ICCA!

I hope that you enjoy reading *Getting Started as an Independent Computer Consultant.* I encourage you to join the ICCA. What a great combination for starting a new consulting business!

Joyce Burkard
Executive Director
Independent Computer Consultants Association (ICCA)
execdirector@icca.org

Introduction

What Is This Book About?

Getting Started as an Independent Computer Consultant is a step-by-step guide to help technology professionals begin their journey toward self-employment. While many computer experts have advanced degrees and years of industry experience, very few have the business skills necessary to start, promote, and manage their own successful consulting practices.

This book is written from an insider's perspective. I will take you through the same journey that I travelled in my quest to become self-employed. All of the basic questions are explored: Should I incorporate? How should I market myself? How much should I charge? What about health insurance? What are the income tax implications?

Who Will Benefit from This Book?

Individuals who have specialized computer skills and the desire to make more money and have more independence will benefit from this book.

Consulting can be a rewarding and lucrative profession. There are hundreds of thousands of consultants in this country working for prestigious firms and making good money. But this book is not about consultants who are employed by consulting firms. This book is about those courageous individuals who seek independence and control over their own lives and schedules. As an independent consultant, you can:

- Make more money;

- Choose which clients you will work for;

- Take more time off;

- Turn down offers for projects that don't interest you; and

- Make your own travel arrangements.

Why Is This Book Different?

There are many excellent books in print that are focused on the consulting business, in general. Yet very few are targeted toward technology professionals. Independent technology professionals are very different from marketing, management, financial, public relations, and other types of consultants.

Most independent technology consultants do not submit proposals or offer specific solutions for their clients. They typically do not meet with their prospective clients face-to-face and explain how their firm or their approach is superior to that of their competitors.

Independent computer consultants are usually brought in on short notice, based on a quick telephone interview and background check. They work on an hourly basis, or what is known in the industry as "time and materials." They usually have a home office. They do not have any full-time employees. Their marketing materials consist of business cards, a website and, maybe, a brochure.

There are four basic ways that independent computer consultants are hired:

- Directly by a client;

- Through another, larger consulting firm;

- By another independent consultant; and

- Through a recruiting agency.

Independent consultants usually rely on their track records (which carry much more weight than college degrees or scholastic achievements) to get lucrative contracts. On the job, they are typically put to work in a cubicle where they build planning models, debug computer programs, or write Java scripts—at very good hourly rates ($50 - $250/hour).

Technology professionals from virtually any industry can profit from this book. The healthcare, government, entertainment, automotive, and construction industries employ thousands of technology professionals. Many computer experts employed in these industries would like to become independent, but some lack the business skills to get started. This is where *Getting Started as an Independent Computer Consultant* can be a huge benefit.

Who Become Independent Computer Consultants?

Most successful independent computer consultants have specialized skills that are in high demand. Many have the following personality traits:

- They are willing to take risks;

- They desire to work on a variety of projects in different industries and locations;

- They want more control over their schedule; and

- They are financially motivated.

The backgrounds of independent computer consultants are very diverse. There are hundreds, if not thousands, of specialties within the computer software industry. Many of today's successful independent consultants come from large consulting firms, such as Accenture and BearingPoint, where they learned how to install, configure, implement, troubleshoot, and maintain software systems. Examples of these types of consultants are:

- ERP consultants (SAP, PeopleSoft, and JD Edwards);

- Business intelligence (BI) consultants (Cognos, Hyperion, and Business Objects); and

- Programming language specialists (Visual Basic, Java, and C-Sharp).

Other independent computer consultants come from software companies, where they have developed new products and enhanced existing ones. Many software companies employ not only developers, but trainers, pre-sales people, and customer service technicians. Examples of software companies that employ computer experts are:

- Microsoft

- IBM

- Oracle

Some independent computer consultants have no consulting experience at all. I know of several very successful independent computer consultants who went from being a business analyst, IT director, or database administrator to starting their own businesses.

Who Hires Independent Computer Consultants?

Many prospective clients actually prefer to hire independent consultants to staff short-term and long-term projects instead of hiring full-time, permanent employees or large consulting firms. Here are a few of the reasons:

- Some employers may have an immediate need to staff a project, and cannot afford to spend time training their own employees.

- Some companies may not be able to locate and attract qualified individuals in their own geographical area.

- Some companies shy away from engaging large consulting firms because they are too expensive.

- The skills required for a project may be so specialized that only a few experts exist nationally.

- Some companies may not be willing to interview, screen, train, and pay benefits to prospective employees who might ultimately leave the company once the project is completed.

These factors have created many lucrative opportunities for independent computer consultants.

How Is This Book Organized?

Getting Started as an Independent Computer Consultant is divided into thirteen chapters. Each chapter covers a specific topic in detail, addressing a major area of starting a computer consulting business. Because I have organized the book this way, you can find the topic you are looking for quickly and easily.

Can You Become an Independent Computer Consultant?

By the time you have finished *Getting Started as an Independent Computer Consultant*, you will have a much clearer idea of what it takes to become an Independent Computer Consultant and thrive as one. Not only will you be better able to assess whether you currently have the skills needed, but you will be able to determine if becoming independent is for you. If it is, this book will help on your way.

CHAPTER 1

Are You Ready?

Do you have a background in technology and the desire to make more money? Do you want more independence? If so, computer consulting may be for you. Consulting can be a rewarding and lucrative profession. There are hundreds of thousands of consultants in this country working for prestigious firms, making good money.

But this book is not about consultants who are employed by consulting firms. This book is about those courageous individuals who seek more freedom and more control over their own lives. I have personally mentored many successful consultants who have followed in my footsteps and have become independent.

Here are just a few of the qualities that most successful independent computer consultants possess:

- Excellent technical skills;
- Willingness to take risks;
- Highly motivated;
- Above average communication skills;
- Above average intelligence; and
- Entrepreneurial mindset.

The Ups and Downs of Self-Employment

Self-employment is not for everyone. For those like me, it is the only career path that works. For others, being employed by corporations is fine, but being self-employed is a step up. Others need the perceived security they find in being employed by corporations and are not suited to self-employment.

Here are some of the benefits of self-employment:

- Prestige. Your friends will be jealous.

- Potential for making a lot of money.

- Variety of assignments.

- Freedom to choose your own schedule.

- Freedom to take time off and plan vacations without having to ask for permission.

- Freedom to express opinions and propose out-of-the-box solutions at work with reduced risk of termination.

- Freedom to choose which projects to accept and which ones to turn down.

While being self-employed is a great way to achieve more independence, it is not perfect. And it is not for everyone. Here are some disadvantages:

- There is no job security.

- There are no company paid benefits such as health insurance, life insurance, and 401(k) matching.

- You may have down time between projects with no income.

- You will incur business expenses such as advertising, supplies, and liability insurance.

- Qualifying for mortgages might be more difficult in the first two years.

- Collecting money from clients can be an issue.
- Most business relationships are short-term.
- Some clients treat their consultants poorly.

For me, becoming self-employed has been the highest and greatest achievement I have ever realized in my career. I continue to reap the benefits. I recommend it to anyone who is willing to take risks and wants to experience more freedom and satisfaction in his or her working life.

> *"Whatever course you decide upon, there is always someone to tell you that you are wrong. There are always difficulties arising which tempt you to believe that your critics are right. To map out a course of action and follow it to an end requires courage."*
>
> —*Ralph Waldo Emerson*

The Personality of an Entrepreneur vs. the Personality of an Employee

Most of us have been employees at one time or another. I have worked for both large and small corporations. When I was twenty-four, I worked as a payroll clerk for slightly more than minimum wage. I worked hard, went to school at night, and tried to adapt to corporate life.

By the time I was twenty-nine, I had earned an MBA and was the controller and chief financial officer of a plastics company. I thought that I had achieved the pinnacle of success in life.

But things happening at work made me question my career choice. I am sure that most of you have experienced at least some of the following:

- I resented having to ask for permission to leave work early or to take a vacation.

- I felt that the only way I could make more money was to change jobs.

- I did not like being told how to do things.

- My efforts were not always appreciated.

- Some of my superiors were difficult to work with and unreasonable.

- I had jobs with virtually no opportunity for promotion or advancement.

- I was locked into some jobs for years because my stock options or 401(k) matching had vesting schedules.

- I was ill-equipped for and unwilling to participate in office politics.

- I was sometimes given unreasonable deadlines that required me to work overtime and weekends.

- Worst of all, when times were tough, I was laid off.

By the time I reached my mid-thirties, I was already on my way to becoming an entrepreneur. I knew that the only way that I would ever be happy in my career was to become self-employed.

"A good indignation brings out all one's powers."

—*Ralph Waldo Emerson*

I started doing consulting on the side. I lived in Silicon Valley (San Francisco Bay Area) and helped entrepreneurs write business plans and raise venture capital. I assisted two startup companies in obtaining millions of dollars in seed money.

I wrote and self-published a book titled, *Accounting Software Guide*. I also started a software company, publishing income tax software. I even did a series of seminars on my own titled, *Accounting for Non-Accountants*.

My early attempts at becoming self-employed were met with some successes and some failures. After each business failure, I found myself reentering the workforce as an accountant or salesperson. It was very discouraging and frustrating at times. I thought I had done all the right things, yet long-term success as an entrepreneur seemed to elude me.

But I never lost sight of my goal to become self-employed. It wasn't until I was in my late forties that I became truly independent. It was computer consulting that helped me get there.

Misconceptions about What It Takes to Be Successful

Computer consulting is hard work. It is a detail oriented business that sometimes requires long hours and a great deal of persistence.

Many newly independent computer consultants give up on self-employment during the first year. Some are not used to negotiating terms, collecting money, and marketing themselves. Many highly qualified computer experts end up going back to their previous careers as permanent, full-time employees.

The following qualifications are typically *not enough* to be successful as an independent computer consultant:

- College degrees;
- Technical certificates;
- Industry certificates;
- Superior intelligence;
- Years of experience;
- Willingness to work hard;
- Ability to follow instructions; and
- Specialized skills.

These qualifications will increase your likelihood of success as an employee of an organization, but they do not automatically ensure your success as an independent consultant.

Successful independent computer consultants see themselves as entrepreneurs first and technicians second. Their desire to be independent exceeds their need for security. While they are concerned about cash flow issues and being without income for periods of time, they are willing to risk short-term losses in order to make more money and have more career satisfaction in the long-term.

The decision to become an independent computer consultant is a very personal one. I have been approached by many firms over the past few years and asked to join them as a full-time employee. Some of the offers are tempting. But, at least for now, I prefer to have the freedom and satisfaction of being self-employed.

> *"Never be afraid to try something new.*
> *Remember, amateurs built the ark; professionals built the Titanic."*
>
> —*Author Unknown*

Five Critical Questions to Ask Yourself

Here are five critical questions you should ask yourself before jumping out on your own:

1. Are there enough prospective clients in your geographical area to support a full-time consulting business?

2. If not, are you willing to travel for long periods of time to client sites to earn income?

3. Are you willing and financially able to go without income for weeks, and even months, while you are looking for new projects?

4. Are the hourly consulting rates in your area of expertise high enough to compensate you for the loss of medical insurance, retirement, and other benefits?

5. Do you know of others in your field who have successfully made the transition from employee to independent contractor?

Are There Enough Clients?

I live in the Denver, Colorado area. As of this writing, I have been an independent computer consultant for over seven years. In those seven years, I have only done two projects in the State of Colorado. One project was a two-week engagement; the other was for only one day. I travel out of state to do the bulk of my work.

I specialize in business intelligence software. More specifically, I build financial forecasting models. Knowing how to build these complex models takes a long time to learn and requires superior skills in finance, configuration, model building, databases, and operating systems. In fact, my skills are so specialized that there are only a handful of independent consultants who compete with me.

When potential clients seek an experienced, independent business intelligence consultant, most of them cannot find local talent. These potential clients usually have to bring in consultants from outside their geographical area. Because the product is so complex and there is a shortage of qualified independent consultants who are willing to travel 100% of the time, I usually have no problem landing lucrative contracts.

Obviously, if you live in a densely populated area like Los Angeles, Houston, Chicago, or Atlanta, you are much more likely to have local clients. However, if you live in a more remote area like New Hampshire, Montana, Alabama, or Nebraska, it is very likely that you will have to travel outside your home state in order to keep busy and be successful.

Are You Willing to Travel?

There is no doubt about it, business travel is tough. I have been doing it for more than eight years. It is exhausting and it is hard on a family. The divorce rate for traveling consultants is much higher than for those who do not travel. It is difficult to have any sort of life in your own community if you are gone thirty-five to forty-five weeks a year.

Here are some factors that helped me deal with the constant travel:

- I make over $100,000 a year—far more than I can make at any full-time job in Denver, where I live.

- I only work about thirty-five weeks a year, which means I have seventeen weeks of vacation.

- I earn hundreds of thousands of frequent flyer miles every year, a tax-free benefit that allows me and my family to go to fabulous places such as Hawaii, Puerto Vallarta, Palm Springs, and Orlando—for free.

- I earn hundreds of thousands of hotel points every year, another tax-free benefit that enables me and my family to stay at the best hotels—for free.

- I have attained elite status with many airlines, which entitles me to perks such as free upgrades to first class, priority boarding, priority seat selection, and bonus miles.

- I have attained elite status with Hilton and Marriott hotels, which entitles me to free room upgrades, guaranteed availability when rooms are sold out, and bonus points.

- I have purchased (and deducted for business purposes) services such as a membership to United's Red Carpet Club and a Clear card, which expedites my journey through security lines at many airports.

- I live in the Denver area, which is right in the middle of the country and a hub for United Airlines and Frontier Airlines.

I can get to just about every major city in North America in three or four hours.

- I have a wife and a son who are very understanding about my business and appreciate the material and emotional benefits of having me as a husband and father.

Later, I will review ways that you can make business travel more tolerable. This includes obtaining elite status with multiple airlines, as well as purchasing services that you can deduct as business expenses.

Are You Willing to Go Without Income While Looking for Projects?

Unfortunately, there may be times when there just are not any projects out there, of any duration and in any location, even at discounted rates.

I have, at times, gone for two or three months with no income coming in. It is a scary proposition, one that drives my wife crazy. It is during these difficult times that I question my self-worth, think about changing careers, and question why I didn't try to work more hours at my last project.

For me, the end of the world is always thirty days away. I am constantly promoting myself, making business connections, and talking to recruiters, regardless of how busy I am. Even if you are on a very lucrative long-term project, you should never curtail your self-promotion campaigns.

This is where many independent computer consultants fall flat on their faces. They are so busy working that they lose sight of their long-term strategies and fail to maintain their business relationships or professional connections.

If the thought of going for three months at a time with no income is unacceptable to you, then reconsider your decision to become an independent computer consultant.

If you decide to proceed and become independent, manage your finances so you can survive during the tough times. This topic is covered in more detail in Chapter 13.

Are Consulting Rates High Enough?

The value of company sponsored benefit plans can be enormous. Some companies offer profit sharing, stock options, robust medical coverage, and other wonderful benefits. These benefits can be very difficult to walk away from, especially if you are on a vesting schedule.

A good friend of mine anguished about his decision to go independent for years. He described, in detail, his company's many benefits, including rewards for longevity, such as four or five weeks of paid vacation a year and 100% 401(k) matching. He hated his job intensely, but just could not seem to bring himself to resign. He had a wife and two small children.

Finally, after four long years of my mentoring and coaching, he quit his job and became an independent contractor. After a few months on his own, he went back to work as a full-time, permanent employee of another large company. Independent consulting, he discovered, was not for him.

Before you make the decision to become an independent consultant, you should carefully weigh the pros and cons of this very significant career change. If you are employed by a company, most of your company benefits are either tax free or tax deferred. Your decision to walk away from these benefits should be well planned and well thought out.

As a general rule of thumb your hourly consulting rate should be at least double your hourly rate with an employer. Let's say you are making $80,000 a year. Using a forty-hour work week as a guide, there are 2080 hours in a year. And $80,000 divided by 2080 is around $40. If you are unable to charge at least $80 an hour as a consultant, then you should reconsider your decision to become independent.

Why should your independent consulting rate be double your hourly rate with an employer? Because you must take into account benefits you will have to provide for yourself, the cost of doing business, and downtime.

In addition to factoring in the loss of health insurance, 401(k) matching, life insurance, and other benefits, you will not be working 2080 billable hours. Some time will be diverted to marketing efforts, billing, and other business management activities. Some time will be lost to downtime. Not only is it extremely unlikely that you will have 2080 billable hours in any given year, you will be very fortunate to have 1500 billable hours. In my first full year as an independent computer consultant, I billed less than 1000 hours.

When I first became independent, my billing rate was $75 an hour. I actually made less money in my first year of consulting than I would have if I had stayed a full-time employee. Many independent consultants experience similar results. It may take you a while to establish yourself as an expert, which will impact the hourly rate you can reasonably charge. However, you should be able to command higher rates over time, as you establish yourself and your expertise.

There are some exceptions. I know of a few individuals who were making more money than me on their first gig.

Later in the book, I will review strategies for obtaining health insurance, life insurance, and establishing your own retirement plan.

Have Others Made the Transition?

You should definitely avoid being a "pioneer" in your field, someone who goes where none have ventured before.

I was a pioneer in my field. In May of 2001, I became the first independent Adaytum consultant. (Adaytum Corporation was acquired by a large software company in 2003). Adaytum was a small company that specialized in financial forecasting software. Their consultants were being billed out for around $200 an hour. I worked as an Applications Consultant for them.

When I left the company, there *were* no independent Adaytum consultants. I felt I could build a business charging $75 an hour for my services. My initial goal was to make $68,000 a year, which was what I had made at Adaytum.

Things were going well until September 11, 2001. I had just finished a project in Wisconsin and was actively looking for my next project. I woke up that morning to find that the world had changed.

I struggled for the next few months. Then, in February, 2002, my phone started ringing. I landed a series of lucrative projects, three of them back-to-back. The third one lasted for six months. I knew I was on my way.

I was at a great disadvantage when I first started out. Since there was no such thing as an independent Adaytum consultant at the time, I had to reassure potential clients that it was okay to hire me. Eventually, the concept took off and it became easier for me to get gigs. More people left Adaytum and became independent consultants. That gave me more credibility—and the precedent I had set no doubt gave them credibility, too. But I was the trailblazer.

For me, personally, 2002 and 2003 were pretty good years. In 2003, I got my hourly rate up to $90 and worked twenty-four weeks that year. I netted about $80,000. At the end of 2003, I created my own website, www.mitchpaioff.com. That marketing strategy really launched my business into high gear. I am always surprised by how few independent consultants have their own websites. Having a website can take your business to the next level.

By 2004, I was charging in excess of $100 an hour and making well over $100,000 a year. I have made over $100,000 a year ever since.

I would not recommend becoming a trailblazer. You are much better off entering a field where others are already making good money. If you know of individuals with backgrounds similar to yours who are successful as independent consultants, you have confirmation that there is an established need in the marketplace for people with your skill set.

* * *

Take the time to consider the strategic, financial, emotional, and mental implications of being an independent consultant before you take the plunge. Are you suited to the lifestyle? Are you comfortable taking risks? Are you willing to do the marketing necessary for your business to flourish? Is there evidence that companies need consultants with your skill set? If you have examined your own readiness to become independent and have decided to go forward, then identifying your niche is the next step.

Identifying Your Niche

There are many specialties within the computer consulting industry. Some offer more opportunities and command higher rates than others.

I specialize in building complex financial forecasting models. My clients use these models to create annual budgets and rolling forecasts. Being a financial modeling consultant requires skills in finance, databases, and operating systems, in addition to the software product itself. I have worked to differentiate myself from all of the other financial modeling consultants out there. Here are a few reasons why I have been so successful:

- I have a website, www.mitchpaioff.com.

- I have developed my own training materials for the financial modeling software product in which I specialize.

- I keep in touch with my former clients on a regular basis and let them know when I am available.

- I keep in touch with the consulting firms and agencies I have worked for in the past.

- I keep a database of potential clients and call them occasionally, even when I am working.

The most lucrative specialties in the computer consulting industry tend to be the "new, hot things." During the late 1990s, many independent ERP (Enterprise Resource Planning) consultants were making over $100 an hour. Back then, if you knew anything about how to configure

SAP, JD Edwards, BAAN, or PeopleSoft, you could go just about anywhere and make a ton of money.

By 2000 and 2001, most of the low hanging fruit in the ERP industry had been picked. Hundreds of independent ERP consultants were competing with each other for fewer projects. Software companies such as JD Edwards were downsizing. Hourly consulting rates dropped significantly. Some consulting firms went out of business.

Follow the Demand

There are virtually thousands of niches today in which qualified computer consultants can command high hourly rates. As a financial modeling consultant, my skills are so specialized that many companies are willing to pay me $100 an hour or more plus travel expenses to come to their offices and work on their systems.

The main disadvantage of my business is that I am becoming *too* specialized. After working on just one software product for over eight years, I am not really qualified to do anything else. The projects that become available every year are limited. And each year many new, bright consultants come into this field to compete with me for those few projects.

Here are some tips for identifying the "new, hot thing":

- Talk to recruiters and ask them which specialties are the hardest for them to fill.

- Do key word searches on job websites and check out the ones with the most opportunities.

- Read trade publications on upcoming trends in your area of expertise.

The highest hourly rates are paid when the supply and demand equation is out of balance. If there is a shortage of qualified workers for a given skill and the demand is high, the rates go up. The downside comes when more new consultants enter a "hot" field over time. What has gone up now comes down. More players in the field means lower rates.

Certifications

One way to gain an edge over other consultants in a competitive field is to get certified. In my opinion, certifications are very beneficial for someone just starting out. However, once you have established yourself as an expert in a given area, your track record and accomplishments are much more important than certifications. Very few of my prospects even ask me if I am certified.

Having a certification by itself will not do much for your consulting career. There are two main reasons that companies hire consultants: experience and leadership. (This will be covered more fully later.) Without the experience, certificates will not be of much use.

How to Get Experience

If you are not already an expert in some area with growing demand, there are some basic ways to get the experience necessary to become an independent computer consultant. These are:

- Get hired by a software company. I got my start in consulting by working as a trainer for JD Edwards (a large software company) in 1998 and 1999. Then I worked as a consultant for Adaytum (a small software company) from 2000 to 2001. That experience helped me get consulting jobs as an independent.

- Get hired by a consulting firm.

- Get hired by a company that uses the technology in which you eventually want to specialize. Many independent consultants are former IT managers, business analysts, and technology experts who have worked for companies that have implemented systems internally.

Once you get hired by one of these firms, sign up for as many training courses as you can. Volunteer to do difficult projects. Take leadership roles whenever possible. Get certified.

While many independent consultants start out working as consultants for either consulting firms or software companies, I do know several very successful independent consultants who became independent without ever having worked as a consultant or for a software company. In most cases, these were IT people who had worked for companies that had done implementations using consultants and they had supervised the consultants on the project. They honed their consulting skills during these projects.

Retooling

The pace of technological change today is so rapid that it is often difficult to keep up with all of the innovations. In the mid-1990s, I found that my skills working with Novell networks and small accounting software packages were outdated.

I lucked out in 1998 when I was hired by JD Edwards as a trainer. JD Edwards was a software company that specialized in ERP (Enterprise Resource Planning) systems. I was in the perfect place at the perfect time. JD Edwards was headquartered in Denver, just a few miles from my house. The company was in an unprecedented growth and hiring mode, the result of the Y2K, the Year 2000 phenomena that was prompting many companies to upgrade their software systems.

The fact that my wife was the accounts payable supervisor at JD Edwards made it easy for me to get interviews. She provided me with the names and telephone numbers of hiring managers.

JD Edwards was hiring hundreds of people, for everything from programmers to salespeople. As a trainer, I spent the first few weeks attending classes and learning the software. The company was willing to train new employees from scratch, which was just what I needed. JD Edwards was a well known brand name, and the demand for skilled JD Edwards consultants was very high.

I eventually left JD Edwards to become a consultant, but I could never have become as successful as I am without undergoing some sort of "retooling." JD Edwards was the perfect launching pad for me.

Retooling can be a long, difficult process. If your skills are outdated, you may need to go through a retooling process to increase your value in the marketplace. I spent three years learning JD Edwards and Adaytum software before I even thought about becoming an independent consultant.

The best ways to retool are: 1) get a job with a consulting firm, 2) get a job with a software company, and 3) get a job with a company that uses the software product that you would like to specialize in.

But there are some potential downsides to taking this retooling approach:

- The technology you are learning might be too specialized, making it difficult to find potential clients.

- The technology you are learning might have a short "shelf life" and you could end up retooling on yet another technology down the road. Every technology has a maturing cycle, some longer than others. As more people learn the technology and enter the field as consultants, hourly rates come down.

- Your employer might insist that you sign a restrictive noncompete agreement that could limit or impede your prospects for starting an independent consulting business when you leave the company.

Noncompete Covenants

If you are offered a position with a consulting firm or a software company, beware of noncompete agreements. Many agencies and consulting firms ask you to sign an agreement that forbids you from soliciting their clients. That is to be expected.

The problem occurs when you sign an agreement that forbids your working for any of your employer's competitors for a year or longer after you leave. That agreement, in effect, may force you to change careers until your noncompete expires.

That is exactly what happened to me when I left JD Edwards in 1999. Even though my employment contract did not have a noncompete clause in it, JD Edwards had agreements with their consulting partners that forbade them from hiring away JD Edwards' employees.

The agreement stated that resellers and consulting partners could not hire any JD Edwards employee within the first six months after the employee left JD Edwards. When I was making plans to leave JD Edwards, none of the consulting partners would even talk to me. So I ended up working for Adaytum, a company that published budgeting and forecasting software. That turned out to be a great career move.

Keep in mind that *everything* is negotiable. I was offered a position with a large consulting firm a few years ago. I reviewed their noncompete agreement and didn't like the wording in a couple of the paragraphs.

I contacted their human resources department and asked them to either change or delete the paragraphs I didn't like. They seemed bewildered and at first refused to make the changes. I told them that I would not accept their offer unless they changed the document. Then they said they would check with their legal department. The legal department proposed some changes, which were fine with me, and the noncompete agreement was changed. The human resources department told me that I was the first candidate to ever ask for a change in that document.

There have been many court cases where rulings by judges have clarified just how enforceable these covenants are. Some courts tend to favor employees when they are sued by their former employers.

If you are working for a company and have signed a noncompete agreement and are concerned about the situation, I recommend that you seek an attorney's advice.

* * *

Identifying your niche is an important way for you to differentiate yourself from your competitors. Know what you are good at. Get the experience necessary to support your claim to expertise. Getting certified can be helpful when you are just starting out as an independent consultant, but it is your track record in your niche that will keep business coming in as you gain experience. And, of course, consider retooling your skills if your experience is dated. Essentially, that means carving out a new niche for yourself.

But once you have carved out a niche for yourself, what kinds of roles are available to you within it? That question will be answered next.

Roles and Projects

When you become an independent computer consultant, you might be presented with opportunities you didn't really expect. My advice is to keep an open mind.

Much of my work involves turnaround projects. Turnaround is a polite term for projects that have been mismanaged or are behind schedule and need help. These are not my favorite projects, but I have done so many of them that I am now considered to be a turnaround expert. The upside is that they can be very lucrative.

Turnaround consultant is just one of the roles I have played as a financial modeling consultant. There are others. Below are several roles, with opinions on which to seek and which to avoid.

Common Independent Consulting Roles

New Implementation Consultant

These projects are usually the highest paying and the most prestigious. They require creativity, vision, excellent communication and presentation skills, and strong leadership skills.

The nice aspects of new implementations are:

- Clients are usually excited about the project and motivated.
- You are not redoing a project that someone else has already started.
- You can truly make a positive impact on an organization.
- New implementations have a high probability for success.

Here are some examples of new implementations:

- Implementing an ERP system (Oracle, SAP) for an insurance company.
- Building a data warehouse for a distribution company.
- Implementing a patient management system for a hospital.
- Implementing a point-of-sale system for a chain of retail stores.
- Designing financial forecasting models for a public utility.

These projects are typically very high profile, so success is critical. Bad implementations can harm your reputation, regardless of who is at fault.

Turnaround Consultant

As I have just mentioned, implementations sometimes go awry for a number of reasons. These situations actually create opportunities for consultants to come in and turn a bad situation into a good one.

Some clients tend to blame consultants for bad outcomes, regardless of how well the consultants have performed. It takes a highly skilled consultant to salvage a bad implementation. These assignments tend to be very challenging.

Before you accept a turnaround assignment, press your prospective client for the reasons behind the failure. I have turned down a few of these opportunities because I felt the challenge was either too great or the situation too risky. Remember, when projects go bad, the consultant always gets blamed, regardless of who really is at fault.

Scoping and Proposal Preparation for a Fee

Some consulting firms are presented with opportunities for which they need an outside expert to help them scope or analyze the project and prepare a proposal for submittal to the client.

These assignments are generally only one or two days in length. However, if you do a good job on the scoping and proposal, most firms will hire you to do the actual project. These projects can really test your leadership and creativity skills. Your input can determine whether or not the company that hired you will get the contract.

Scoping, Proposal Preparation, and Presentations for Free

Occasionally I am approached by a consulting firm that does not have money in their budget to pay for my expertise in assisting them with a scoping exercise or a proposal.

My agreement to do this work gratis depends on how busy I am. If I am not working, I am usually more open to it. The benefit of helping these consulting firms is that they will probably hire you, if and when they get a contract and assuming you did a good job on the proposal. It also gets you known within the firm.

I landed one of my most lucrative projects this way. I was asked by a large consulting firm to fly to Texas to meet with a prospective client. I was in between projects at the time. The consulting firm needed an outside technical expert to make the presentation to the client because their own technical expert was out on an assignment and could not be pulled in.

I did the presentation and the client was blown away. The consulting firm got the contract, hired me, and everything turned out great. My being so instrumental in getting the deal put me in a superior bargaining position with the consulting firm. I negotiated a very good rate and terms.

I am often asked to participate in conference calls to help get deals done. Regardless of how busy I am, I am usually open to doing these for free. If the consulting firm gets the job, I usually benefit. Everyone wins.

Training

Though short-term in nature, these assignments are generally the highest paying on an hourly basis. I typically charge $125 to $150 an hour, plus expenses, for a three-day training project. It is a good idea to develop your own training materials in advance and have them ready in anticipation of getting a training assignment. This can be very time consuming, but even if you do only one or two training projects a year, they are lucrative enough to be worth your preparation time.

As a general rule, your rates for short-term engagements should be high. For longer-term engagements, I tend to be more flexible with my rates.

System Administration/Interim Management/Staff Augmentation

Some opportunities arise when companies have employee turnover. Examples of turnover are:

- A project manager leaves a company on short notice;
- A system administrator goes on maternity leave; or
- A reorganization or acquisition creates a vacuum in the IT department.

These situations can either be short-term or long-term. There is typically a sense of urgency when these opportunities arise, so many clients are willing to pay reasonable hourly rates for the right consultant with the right skills, especially if the consultant is available to start immediately. That said, these opportunities tend to have lower hourly rates associated with them. Quite honestly, I don't like these projects because they are usually boring.

Help Desk/Post Implementation Support

These opportunities are by far my least favorite. Some large companies outsource help desk, support, and other day-to-day functions to consulting firms on a permanent basis. The term "managed services" is often used to describe these functions.

These assignments usually involve dealing with problems as they occur. Many companies have strict criteria, such as a fifteen-minute response time to user issues. So you might spend several hours sitting around doing nothing, then be stressed out when five high-priority problems occur within the span of a few minutes. If problems are not resolved quickly, your performance and abilities are questioned.

* * *

If you are offered a project to fill a role with which you are unfamiliar, my advice would be to take a chance on it. It may open up many doors for you in the future.

Specializing vs. Diversifying

Some consultants have skills in multiple areas and try to market themselves accordingly. In my opinion, an independent consultant should specialize in one technology.

When I left JD Edwards, my goal was to become an independent JD Edwards consultant. I did one JD Edwards project and then was hired by Adaytum as an applications consultant. I became an Adaytum expert.

After I left Adaytum, I thought about doing both JD Edwards and Adaytum consulting. What I found was that in the year-and-a-half since leaving JD Edwards, the technology had changed significantly. Furthermore, most employers were reluctant to hire me because my experience was not current. New versions had been released. My skills were outdated.

I became an independent Adaytum consultant.

Even so, a few years ago, I was looking for work when I was approached by a local (Denver-based) company looking for a contractor to do an activity based costing (ABC) project. I had some experience in ABC, but did not consider myself an expert. I explained this to the agency. They wanted to hire me anyway. I ended up working there for four weeks. The rate was lower than I was used to, but I was glad to be working and making money. The client was very happy with the work I did there.

I would still recommend staying with one technology. However, when presented with projects outside your primary area of expertise, you might consider accepting them to keep money coming in.

Hiring Subcontractors to Work for You

I hired subcontractors once and it worked out great. In 2002, I was so busy that I was turning away work. I advertised on Monster® (www.monster.com) and found someone who was about to leave his full-time job. I offered to hire him as my subcontractor. I disclosed to him that there was no guarantee I could keep him busy full-time, but I would try.

I billed him out for $115 an hour and paid him $75 an hour. That equates to a $40 an hour margin for me, or $1600 a week profit. After a few weeks, he realized that he could go out on his own, which he did. He is now a very successful independent computer consultant—so successful, in fact, that he makes more money than me.

The two main downsides of hiring subcontractors are risk and cash flow. If your subcontractor does a bad job, you might not be able to collect some or all fees from your client for your contractor's labor. If your client delays payments to you (this happened to me), you still have to pay your subcontractor. I remember at one point I was out $16,000 of my own money while I waited for my client to pay me. I ended up making a lot of money using a subcontractor, but the risks and cash flow problems make it an option I do not prefer.

* * *

Knowing your niche and understanding what roles you can—and choose—to fill are important. But as important as these things are, they will not, in and of themselves, provide lucrative work. What's missing? Marketing. Without the knowledge and willingness to market yourself effectively, you will not have the financially rewarding lifestyle you want. It is the one thing that separates successful independent computer consultants from those who only dream of being successful.

How to Market Yourself Effectively

Independent computer consultants play varied roles in varied settings, as described in the last chapter. But how do they *get* those assignments in the first place?

The two main reasons why companies hire consultants are experience and leadership. Companies are willing to pay a good deal of money to outsiders who can provide solutions to problems they cannot solve themselves. Many are looking for a specific end result. They are not looking for bureaucrats. They have plenty of those. They need skilled professionals who: have vision and can think creatively; can work independently and efficiently; demonstrate initiative and the ability to get the job done; are assertive and can take charge of challenging situations . . . and, at the same time, who can adapt to the company's corporate culture.

But experience and leadership without marketing is like having the lights turned off at a brick and mortar business. You will probably not be found. If you are, it will be by accident. Market well. That means having a Unique Selling Proposition, prospecting for leads, advertising, selling yourself well, and employing other marketing tactics.

Create Your Own USP (Unique Selling Proposition)

As an independent consultant, you must reassure your prospects that you are capable of helping them achieve their objectives. Clearly and briefly state what you do, without a lot of explanation.

This is where your USP comes in.

The Unique Selling Proposition (also Unique Selling Point) is a marketing concept that was first proposed as a theory to explain strategies used in successful advertising campaigns of the 1940s and 1950s. The theory states that such campaigns made unique propositions to customers and that these convinced them to switch brands. A number of businesses (and consultants) use USPs as a basis for their marketing campaigns.

Examples of Famous USPs

Try to guess the name of the company for each of these Unique Selling Propositions:

"Fresh hot pizza in thirty minutes or its free."

"When your package absolutely, positively has to get there overnight."

Sample USPs for Independent Computer Consultants

Here are some good examples of computer consulting USPs:

"I do implementation and training on Hyperion Planning software."

"I implement and configure SAP ABAP systems."

"I build data warehouses using Business Objects."

What Is Your USP?

Your USP should be short and to the point. Avoid trying to be all things to all people. Your clients will pay good money for specialists to come in and solve their specific problems, but they do not want a jack-of-all-trades.

When a recruiter or prospective client asks you what you do, give them your USP. Memorize it! Your USP should be limited to fifteen words or less. By the way, the aforementioned sample USPs in this chapter belong to Domino's Pizza and Federal Express.

What is *your* USP?

Good Sources for Leads

Even though I have been an independent computer consultant for over seven years, I am almost embarrassed to tell you that about 30% of my business comes from my résumé postings on the following websites:

- Monster.com
- Dice.com
- Careerbuilder.com
- Computerjobs.com
- Indeed.com

I am sure that you already know about these websites (and more), right? I just have a few tips:

- Update your profiles frequently. This will help your résumé show up higher in searches by recruiters.
- Do not waste your money "upgrading" your posting for a fee. It probably will not make any difference in your response rates.
- Always include a cover letter when applying for positions online. Your cover letter should be brief. Just tell them that you are interested in the opportunity, explain why you are qualified, and let them know when you can start. If you have a website, direct them to that site in your cover letter. Having a website will impress them and put you miles ahead of your competition.

Great Sources for Leads

My most lucrative contracts have not come from résumé websites. They have come from referrals, my own website, cold calling, and consulting firms seeking contractors.

Referrals

Once you become an independent consultant, you need to hang around with, communicate with, and seek the advice of other independent consultants, especially those in your field. Take them to lunch, send them relevant articles, and call them periodically to see how they are doing. Share stories with them and let them in on what's happening in your industry.

Here are just a few of the benefits of building long-term relationships with other consultants:

- You can compare information you have gathered on consulting rates.

- If they are between projects, you can offer to help them find work. In turn, some of them (but not all) will help you when you are between projects.

- If you have worked with them, they can be references for you.

- They can be technical resources for you when you have issues or problems at work.

- They may know about upcoming projects that have not been advertised.

- They can introduce you to recruiters, project managers, and other key individuals who can help you.

One of the many rewards of being an independent consultant has been sharing my experiences with others in my field. Being away from home and working long hours is tough. But knowing that others are doing the same kind of work is sometimes comforting.

Unfortunately, not all consultants are open and supportive. The consulting business is very competitive and some consultants are paranoid about losing their clients to others. This has actually happened to me—twice. Both times, competitors convinced my clients to fire me and hire them. Many independent computer consultants are justifiably very secretive about their businesses because of such behavior.

If other consultants don't return your phone calls or are otherwise unfriendly, don't take it personally. Many consultants are understandably protective about what they do.

I have helped a number of my protégés obtain lucrative consulting projects and I have never asked for a dime of compensation. Goodwill has a way of returning to you.

Example 1: A former co-worker of mine was laid off a few years ago. She lived on the West Coast. I helped her get a lucrative long-term consulting project with a pharmaceutical company there. A few months later, she and her husband moved to the East Coast. Within a month of her move there, I helped her get a short-term project within driving distance of her house. That project provided her with cash flow while she looked for something more long term. She is a brilliant consultant and has frequently helped me out when things got tough on my own projects.

Example 2: Many years ago, I hired a consultant to work for me and gave him a start as an independent consultant. A couple of years later, I had finished a project and was looking for another one. Around that time, my friend was approached by a consulting firm and they asked him to work for them. He was unavailable so he referred them to me. That referral turned into tens of thousands of dollars in income for me and led to multiple lucrative consulting projects.

Example 3: A couple of years ago, another consultant friend of mine was looking for work. I was doing a search on the Internet one day and happened to find an opportunity right in the small town where he lived. I told him about the opportunity, which was only two miles from his house. The result was a year-long job for him and while he was there, he arranged for his client to hire me to do some in-house training. I charged them $150/hour and they were thrilled with my classes.

By giving and receiving referrals, you and your associates can get the best projects at the highest rates. These opportunities are generally not advertised, so you usually do not need to worry about competition or even providing references.

Create a Website

Because the consulting industry is very competitive, anything you do to differentiate yourself from the competition can give you a significant competitive advantage.

In 2003, I was finally beginning to make serious money as an independent consultant. Word got around about my success and I believe that some people in my field of expertise were jealous. Someone or some group of people started a rumour that I was not certified in the software on which I was working.

I wanted the world to know that I was certified, so I decided to create my own website. That would enable anyone to view my certificate online. Around that same time, I began asking for and receiving letters of recommendation from my clients. I posted those on my website as well. (Go to: www.mitchpaioff.com).

Over time, I added more content to my website. I posted details on my training classes. I posted images of the certificates I received from courses I have taken. All of this has added to my credibility. There is also a list of my many satisfied clients and endorsements from clients.

Whenever I am approached with new consulting opportunities, I refer my prospects to my website. Every email I send them has a link to my website. Here are some benefits I have realized as a direct result from having a website:

- Some prospects who see my letters of recommendation online do not even bother asking for references.

- At the same time, my clients who have provided endorsements are happiest when they are not taking calls about me from prospective clients. People are busy. The website letters of reference respect the time of clients who have been kind enough to endorse me.

- Some prospects have hired me without going through a series of phone interviews.

- If I am driving or at an airport, I can direct prospects who call to my website. If they want a copy of my résumé, they can download it without me actually having to send it to them. That speeds up their decision process.

There are many high-volume website design companies out there that will build your website for a few hundred dollars. Be sure to ask them if they have online editing capabilities. This allows you to update your website yourself, using plain text, without having to know html or other web editing languages.

Once you have a website, load it with content so it will appear on Internet searches for free. I have loaded up my website with dozens of repeat phrases of keywords that describe what I do. For example, you might use "Oracle Financials" or "SAP MMPP." I also have a lot of links going in and out of my website to increase its visibility with search engines like Google.

There are companies that will help you with Search Engine Optimization, or SEO. They can give you tips on how to have your website appear higher up on search engine searches.

Internet Advertising

Of course, once you have a website, you can also advertise online. With Google AdWords, for instance, you can create a marketing campaign in just a few minutes. Here's how it works:

- Create an account at www.Google.com;
- Create ad campaigns based on keywords (such as "Hyperion Planning consultant");
- Set bid amounts of how much you are willing to pay on a per-click basis;
- Set daily limits of how much you are willing to spend.

Once you start advertising with Google, you can view real-time reports on your activity. You can "pause" your campaigns if you are not looking for work. You can "resume" them later when you need them.

I have not had great success with this method. But over the years, I have had a handful of companies hire me for short-term projects. The amount of money I made on those projects was well worth the few hundred dollars I paid to Google.

Example: A few years ago, my wife and I decided to go to Mexico on vacation after I finished a project. We purchased the tickets and made hotel reservations.

I was running an ad on Google. A few days before we were to leave for Mexico, I received an urgent call from a company based in Canada. They saw my ad and needed someone to build them a financial forecasting model.

I asked them, "Can this wait until after next week?"

They said "No, we need you next week."

I quoted them my standard rate of $125/hour, plus expenses. They said, "That's fine."

So I cancelled the trip to Mexico and spent two weeks with this company, working on their forecasting model. I made $10,000 in two weeks. I told my wife that I would make up the lost trip to her.

While I was on that project, another company called me from the same ad and asked, "Can you come out right away and do some onsite training for us?"

I said, "Sure."

I quoted them $135/hour plus expenses. (I always quote higher rates for training engagements because they are usually short-term).

They said, "Come on out."

I worked there for three days and made $3000.

Both of those projects were a direct result of my Google ads. I made $13,000 in three weeks. That pays for a lot of Google ads.

Instead of going to Mexico, my wife and I eventually went to Hawaii and we had a fabulous time.

Conferences

Attending software conferences can be a great way to meet potential clients. Many of these conferences offer formal networking sessions where attendees with similar interests can gather at the same tables for breakfast, lunch and dinner.

Recently, I attended a big software conference in Las Vegas. I saw many of my former clients and made a lot of new connections. One of my former clients asked about my availability. I told him I had just finished another project and was looking for work. That five-minute conversation led to a very lucrative three-month contract. It paid for the cost of the conference many times over.

Even if you are an introvert by nature, you need to become an extrovert at these conferences. You should attend the networking sessions with an open mind and talk to as many people as possible. Bring plenty of business cards.

I always dress up for conferences. I want my prospects to see me as if I were showing up to work on a Monday morning. Avoid blue jeans and t-shirts. Making a good impression here can do wonders for your consulting business.

After attending a conference, it is a good idea to follow up on your leads with a quick email or phone call.

Consulting Firms

I have done many lucrative projects for consulting firms. Consulting firms prefer to use their own employees over contractors. However, when they get busy, they sometimes do not have the time or resources to hire permanent employees. That's when they turn to contractors.

Most consulting firms have high ethical standards and are wonderful to work for. Some consulting firms will try to entice you to work for them as a permanent, full-time employee. That is an option you can consider. It is the best scenario for them, but not usually for you, for the following reason: If you are hired at a starting annual salary of, let's say, $92,000, that equates to an hourly rate of around $44 ($92,000/2080 working hours/year). The consulting firm will probably bill you out for $150 to $200 an hour. That is a huge margin for them. Some firms may tell you that there are many opportunities coming up with them in the future. They might promote their fringe benefits, liberal vacation policy, and other advantages of working full-time for their firm.

It would be much more lucrative for you to negotiate a high hourly rate as a subcontractor. Under this scenario, you might be able to charge them $100 an hour. That's quite an increase from $44, even with all of the company benefits.

I have been approached by consulting firms that have wanted to hire me as a full-time employee many times. If they approach me with such an opportunity, but it appears to really be a short-term project, I say to them, "I might be interested in working for you as a full-time employee at some point. What I would recommend is that we do this first project together with me as a contractor. Then we can see if we like each other. I have my own way of doing things and let's make sure that our styles are similar. Once this first project is over, we can discuss my coming on board."

My experience has been that, in most cases, whether you are an employee or a contractor, when the project is over, there will be no additional projects. You would have been laid off either way. You will usually be better off getting the high hourly rate.

The first consulting firm I ever worked for hired me as a permanent, full-time employee. They said they had a "long-term" JD Edwards report writing project in Texas. They assured me that once that project ended, there would be more projects to follow. I quit my job at JD Edwards to work for them.

They put me up in a cheap motel in Dallas and gave me a salary of $65,000 a year (about $32/hour). After nine weeks, the project ended and they laid me off. I received no severance pay. That was ten days before my wedding day. I was unemployed on my wedding day.

You are almost always better off working as an independent contractor at a high hourly rate than as a consulting firm employee.

Recruiting Agencies

Recruiting agencies are companies that locate contractors for specific assignments. Their rates are generally lower than consulting firms. These agencies typically do not have experienced practice managers who monitor your projects to ensure a successful outcome.

I receive a lot of calls from recruiting agencies. Many seem to be price driven, which means that they are looking for consultants with the lowest asking rates. Some try to negotiate a low rate with me before they ever determine whether or not I am available or even qualified for the project.

I have worked for a few of these agencies and they have been great. In two cases, the rate was very good. In one case, the rate was low. All of them conducted themselves professionally and they paid me on time.

When recruiters from agencies call, I am always polite to them. You never know when you will need them.

Selling Yourself over the Telephone

Selling yourself over the telephone is an art. Persistence is the key to success here. You might have to make fifty or more cold calls to get one solid lead. I have acquired many new clients this way. It is definitely not my preferred way, but you should know how to do this, especially when you are between projects and looking for new assignments.

Cold calling is an absolute necessity if you are serious about being a successful independent consultant, but it is a time consuming, frustrating, and monotonous activity. I know no one who likes cold calling. Being successful at cold calling involves:

- Being assertive;

- Having a high tolerance for rejection;

- Being able to quickly respond to objections;

- Knowing when there is a potential opportunity and when there is none; and

- Having the willingness to make mistakes.

The best way to begin your cold calling campaign is to just do it. It may feel uncomfortable at first, but the more you do it, the better you will get at it. You will make mistakes, as I have. Some people will even hang up on you. Be persistent. Some of my best projects came from cold calling.

I started cold calling when I first became an independent consultant. What I did was search job sites like Monster® (www.monster.com) for keywords. When I found an opening for a permanent, full-time employee, I called the company and attempted to reach the hiring manager. If I reached him or her, I asked, "Would you consider bringing in an expert like me on a temporary basis to do some training or to troubleshoot your system?"

Most of the time (98%), the answer was, "No."

However, I did acquire a few good clients this way.

When I am between projects and looking for work, I always do cold calling. Having an opening line and a written script are absolute musts.

Opening Line

Each cold call begins with an opening line. Here is the one I typically use: "Hi, this is Mitch Paioff. May I speak to the person in charge of your financial modeling project?"

Always try to reach the decision maker. Be polite to everyone you talk to, but know that you will never get hired without talking directly to the decision maker. One of your goals when doing cold calling is to at least learn the name of the decision maker. Once you have that person's name, you can always call back later if s/he is not immediately available.

Once you reach the decision maker, either have your script memorized, word-for-word, or written down. *Do not try to wing this!*

Sample Script

"Hi (manager), my name is Mitch Paioff and I am an independent financial modeling consultant. I recently completed a very successful financial modeling implementation at ABC Company. I was looking online and noticed that your company has an opening for a business analyst with financial modeling experience. I was wondering if you might consider bringing in an experienced professional like me to assist with some of your financial modeling projects on a temporary basis?"

Gathering Information and Qualifying the Prospect

If the answer is, "No," which will be the answer you receive about 98% of the time, make a note in your contact management database of who you talked to. Include his/her job title, direct line or cell phone number, email address, when you talked, and what s/he said. Many companies experience high turnover, and while the current manager might not be interested in hiring you at the moment, he or his replacement might need you in six months or a year. Send an email with a link to your website. Offer to check back with him in sixty days.

What to Do When You Find a Good Prospect

If there is interest, try to gather as much information as you can about the prospect's needs. What is the level of pain? Have the decision maker "go deep" into that pain and describe the real consequences of not having an expert like you on board. Are deadlines being missed? Are employees working overtime to fix things? Is not having the right solution costing the company money or missed opportunities?

Once you understand the decision maker's pain, explain how you would be the perfect person to heal it. What outcome is s/he expecting? What is the time frame? Does the company need classroom training?

If the prospect is interested and you feel the timing is appropriate, offer to send the prospect your Consulting Agreement. Do not call it a "Consulting Contract" until s/he has signed it. "Agreement" sounds friendlier than "contract." Also send a résumé, a summary of relevant experience, and a link to your website.

Ask the decision making prospect to "approve" the agreement as opposed to "sign" it. Again, "approve" sounds friendlier than "sign." Ask that the approved agreement be faxed back to you.

When you find an interested prospect, they typically will not question your hourly rate or even ask for references. They may, however, ask you to put a limit on travel expenses. You can offer to put a "not to exceed" limit next to each travel expense item in your agreement addendum. An example would be: "Round trip airfare to and from client's headquarters, not to exceed $900 per trip." You can limit hotels to $180/night, rental cars to $75/day, and meals to $35/day.

Here are the main points to cover when you find a good prospect:

- Find out what the prospect needs. Experience their pain.
  Ask open-ended questions. Listen. Have the prospect "go deep"
  into their pain and describe the awful consequences.

- Discover what the prospect wants you to do. If they are not
  sure, propose an agenda and a timeline for them.

- Reassure the prospect that you are the perfect candidate
  for the job.

- Ask closing questions (see below).

- Offer to send the prospect a "Consulting Agreement."

- With the agreement, send the client your résumé, a summary of
  your recent projects, and a link to your website. Having a great
  website with your photo, a list of previous clients, and some

letters of recommendation can help you to close the deal. It also helps if you are incorporated and have liability insurance.

- Do *not* offer to give your prospect a list of references at this stage. They usually will not ask. If they ask, make sure that you have at least five good references you can email to them. Do not muddle up the process by offering to provide references if they have already decided to hire you.

Closing Questions

When I feel that a prospect is getting close to hiring me, I often ask a series of closing questions. The types of closing questions that I like to ask are what is called "Alternative of Choice."

Samples: "What time would you like me to start on Monday, 8 a.m. or 9 a.m.?"

"When would you like to schedule the classroom training, the week of the 11th or the week of the 18th?"

After you ask a closing question, shut up! Don't say another word! Let the prospect digest the information before he makes a decision. There might be thirty seconds or even three minutes of uncomfortable silence. Don't interrupt the prospect's thought process. Decisions have consequences, and your prospect needs to sort these out before verbally committing.

By asking a closing question, you are making it easy for the prospect to commit to hiring you. This closing technique is used by car, furniture, and insurance sales people . . . and anyone else who is successful in closing deals.

Once the prospect answers a closing question by choosing an option you have proposed, you are done! The rest is just paperwork.

That's the easy part. Now you will have to deliver on your promises.

The Expanding Project

It is quite normal for a project to continue longer than originally planned. This is usually called "scope creep." Scope creep occurs when a client (or consultant) discovers other areas in the organization where you can add value.

The term "scope creep" can have negative connotations. Some clients perceive it as a way consultants extend their assignments and take advantage of a lucrative situation. That has never been the case for me. Many of my clients ask me to extend because they are happy with my work and receive real value from my services.

When you are on a project, you should always try to identify new opportunities for your services. If a client likes you and trusts you, they will often keep you for longer than planned. Exceptions to this are situations in which a client has a tight deadline or a fixed budget. Delivering high quality work will increase your likelihood of staying on with that client.

I was once hired to do an eight-week project with a large consulting firm. That project ended up lasting for eight months!

Keeping Great Clients

Repeat clients are not a major source of income for me, though I know they are for some other independent consultants. I do, however, have repeat business with consulting firms.

When I get repeat business with clients, it is because I did great work for them the first time. A great track record is a great marketing tool. And with the robust turnover at many companies, a great client contact (whether corporate or consulting firm) may leave a company for whom I worked and land in another that needs me. A good track record will get you remembered when that happens.

* * *

If you are technically good at what you do and want both more freedom and more money, becoming independent may seem the natural thing to do. But for many skilled computer professionals, marketing is not second nature. It may be a great fantasy to "build it and they will come." But the real-world difference between those who build their independent consulting businesses and have many well-paying clients and those who build them and wonder where those clients are is marketing.

Learn to love marketing, or at least learn to see it as one of the skill sets you must develop to have a thriving business. Once you do, you will not have to sit back and wait for long because they *will* come.

CHAPTER 5

How Much Should I Charge?

The answer to this question is always: As much as possible!

This is one of the most complicated and difficult aspects of being an independent consultant. All of us want the highest rates with the best terms. But we do not want to price ourselves so high that we are not competitive with other consultants. And if you are trying to get that long-term project, whatever rate you start at will probably end up being your rate for the duration. Once you are on a project, it is very unlikely that your client will give you a raise.

I have read many books on how to become a consultant. Some of these books have proposed mathematical formulas for determining the ideal rate. What I have found is that there *is* no ideal rate. Of course, as discussed earlier, you need to charge enough to cover the cost of health insurance and other benefits you must provide for yourself. You also need to cover the cost of downtime, the time when you are not working. And you need to charge an appropriate rate for your skills and experience. But the market will almost always determine how much you can charge.

Negotiations can be stressful. Here are some things to consider.

First Projects

If you are just starting out as an independent contractor, you may be competing against more experienced consultants. You might consider accepting a lower rate on your first two or three projects to get some experience.

During my first two years as an independent contractor, I averaged about $75/hour. By year three, I was getting around $100/hour. Since then, I have averaged $115 to $120/hour, but have had many projects that paid $125/hour and even higher than that.

Multiple Choices in Good Times

If you are being sought after by a number of recruiters, you have a lot more leverage in negotiations. When choosing which project to accept, you should consider important factors in addition to the rate. Location, starting date, and/or the flexibility to do some work from home may be important to you and can all be negotiated.

Honesty is the Best Policy

Be honest when you are approached by a recruiter and asked, "What is your availability?"

If you are in the final stages of a negotiation with another firm, you can tell the recruiter, "I am available right now, but that could change. I am being considered for another project. I cannot guarantee my availability until I have an actual contract with you."

A few years ago, I was negotiating with two recruiters for different projects at around the same time. I was honest with both of them and told them I was being considered for another project. Company #1 sent me a written offer first. About twenty minutes later, Company #2 called and said they were sending me an offer. I told Company #2 that I had just signed a contract with another firm. They were very disappointed. But because I had been honest with them all along, they hired me to work on another project a few months later.

Seasonality

I have been a financial modeling consultant for a number of years and have experienced a predictable seasonality factor in my business. The "high season" for me is February through September. That is when the demand for my skill is at its highest and I can charge premium rates. The "low season" is October through January and I am usually willing to accept lower rates during those months.

Sometimes luck is on your side. In October, 2004, I finished a project and there were very few opportunities available. I assumed my working year was over and expected to hibernate until February. Then in late November, a company called me out of the blue and offered me a three-week project at $125/hr. That made my Christmas a lot merrier.

Long-term vs. Short-term

I typically charge a premium rate for short-term projects and offer a discount for long-term ones. My standard rate for a project of four weeks or less is $125/hr. If I am without work and desperate for it, I will consider taking less for a short-term project.

Long-term projects are different. I will usually consider a discount of, say, $10 to $15/hr. for longer-term projects, depending on location and duration. Beware, though, because some recruiters will tell you that a project's duration will be six months or more when it will really be less than that.

Consulting Firms

If you are being considered by a consulting firm, remember that they have to make enough money from your labor to make the deal worthwhile for them. Consulting firms typically mark up subcontractor rates by 30% or more. So if they are charging their client $125 an hour, it is unlikely that they will pay you $110/hr.

If you are unwilling to work for a lower rate to accommodate the firm's profit margin, then you need to pass on the opportunity. All of the negotiation techniques in the world will not get you a higher rate in such cases.

Terms

My payment terms are net fourteen days. Many consulting firms state that their terms are net thirty days. Some are as much as forty-five days.

Terms are usually negotiable. Most of the time, I get my net fourteen-day terms. On one project, I compromised with a consulting firm whose terms were usually net thirty days. We agreed to net twenty-one. On another project, the firm's terms were also net thirty days. However, through negotiation they agreed to reimburse my travel expenses with fourteen-day terms, and my labor with thirty-day terms.

Terms can be negotiated, but only if you set them in the first place. To meet your own obligations, you must set payment terms or you will be at the whim of the accounts payable department.

Know Your Market

The best way to determine your worth in your field is to know your market. Do your research. Talk to others who are doing what you do. Talk to recruiters. Look for market data online. One place to check out is www.realrates.com. They do consulting rate surveys.

How to Make $100,000 a Year or More

My early goals were modest. When I started out, I would have been thrilled to make $70,000 a year. In my third full year, I made over $100,000. My objective ever since has been to make $100,000 a year. There are many different scenarios that will enable you to make $100,000 a year. Here are a few:

- I typically charge about $120/hour for my services. At that rate, I only need to work about 24 weeks a year to make $100,000 or more ($120/hour x 40 hours/week x 24 weeks/year = $115,200).

- If you charge $80/hour and work 40 weeks/year, that comes to $128,000.

- If you charge $60/hour and work 48 weeks a year, that would be $115,200.

Consider the following factors when estimating your potential net income:

- You will have ongoing expenses that will reduce your net income. These may include advertising, supplies, professional dues, and education.

- You may not be able to work forty hours a week every week.

- If you are leaving a good paying job, you will probably lose your health insurance, retirement benefits, and other benefits. Your rates need to be high enough to compensate you for the loss of these benefits.

- You may need to purchase not only health insurance, but also other insurance policies. You will need to maintain these policies even when you are between projects and not working. Your rates must be high enough to accommodate that.

- Realize that as technologies mature over time, the demand for your skills may subside, bringing down your rates. Also, as more people come into the market, rates tend to drop. This is exactly what happened in 2000 and 2001 in the ERP industry.

* * *

Determining your asking rate is more art than a science. The consultants who are successful at negotiating the highest rates usually have good business skills and a keen awareness of their value in the market.

Can a good living be made as an independent computer consultant? My own experience—and that of those I have mentored—is that it can. Do your homework, consider your value in the market, decide how many hours you want/need to work, and set appropriate rates.

But you will need to do more than set appropriate rates to succeed as an independent computer consultant. You will need to set up your business as a business.

CHAPTER 6

Creating a Business Entity That Works for You

Being an expert in your field, understanding your niche, and being willing to market yourself are all critical to becoming successful as an independent consultant. But before you can actually begin, you need to set up your business.

When you go out on your own, you will probably want to establish yourself as an independent contractor. This means that when you receive payments from your clients, they will not be required to withhold any money from your check.

How you decide to structure your business entity will have a direct and immediate impact on how your income will be taxed.

If you do not incorporate, then you will probably be considered a sole proprietor. Your clients will write checks that are payable to you and you will deposit them in your personal/business checking account. You will report your income and expenses on Schedule C of your federal income tax return. You will be personally liable for any work you do as a sole proprietor. You will also need to pay self-employment taxes on Schedule SE. (See the income tax chapter in this book for more details on self-employment taxes.)

This is the simplest way to start a consulting business. I operated as a sole proprietor for my first two years in business. One risk of operating as a sole proprietor is that the IRS could examine your relationship with your clients and reclassify you as their employee. If the IRS were to audit you or your client and determine that you are, in the eyes of the IRS, an employee rather than an independent contractor, then you or your client could be responsible for payroll taxes and you both could be penalized.

The IRS would rather tax you as an employee. Their reasons for this are simple. As an employee, your payroll taxes and withholding taxes are sent to the IRS immediately, not quarterly or annually. Also, as an employee, you cannot deduct business expenses, such as supplies, on Schedule C of your income tax return.

The IRS looks at the relationship between you and your client to determine whether or not you are truly an independent contractor or an employee. As an independent contractor, you file tax returns and possibly make quarterly estimated payments to the IRS. The IRS has guidelines to determine if the relationship between you and a client is that of employer/employee or client/independent contractor. They use common law rules that fall into three categories: behavioural, financial, and type of relationship. A twenty point test can be applied to determine whether the relationship can be justifiably considered that of client and independent contractor.

The entire relationship is considered and all twenty factors must be taken into consideration to determine the nature of the relationship. There is no magic formula that proves the case one way or the other. Neither a specific number of factors nor one critical factor proves the point. The entire relationship is taken into consideration.

It is important to understand and be able to justify your relationship as an independent contractor. Otherwise you could lose your independent contractor status and have to pay taxes and penalties. Your client could also be at risk. Should you be classified as an employee, your client would have to pay payroll taxes for you.

The Twenty Point Test

1. Instructions

Employees are workers who are required to comply with another person's instructions about when, where, and how they work. A key factor is whether or not the business has retained or surrendered the *right* to control the details of when, where, and how the work is done (as opposed to whether or not they exercise that right). Independent contractors operate using their own procedures and/or industry standards.

2. Training

Providing the worker with training implies that s/he is an employee. It suggests that the job is to be done in a particular way. Training a worker occurs by requiring an experienced employee to work with the worker, by corresponding with the worker, by requiring the worker to attend meetings, or by using other methods to impart knowledge and/or skills. Independent contractors are skilled professionals, are hired for that expertise, and require no training by the client.

3. Integration

To what degree are the worker's services merged and integrated into the business operations? Evidence of direction and control is confirmed by how much the continuation of a business depends upon the performance of certain services. An independent contractor's services are not integral to the business and can stand alone.

4. Services Rendered Personally

Requiring that the services be rendered personally, that is, by a specific person and not delegated, indicates that the person for whom the services are performed is interested in the methods used to accomplish the work, and not simply the results. This suggests an employee relationship.

An independent contractor retains the right to hire others to perform work and/or serve as assistants.

5. Hiring, Supervising, and Paying Assistants

When a business owner hires a worker and then hires assistants for the worker, there is an implied employer-employee relationship between the owner and the worker. If the worker hires his own assistants in order to fulfill a contract with the business owner, the implication is that the worker is an independent contractor.

6. Continuing Relationship

An employer-employee relationship exists if there is a continuing relationship between the worker and the business owner, even if work is performed at irregular intervals. The independent contractor is hired for a specific service/project and the relationship ends when the service/project work has been completed.

7. Set Hours of Work

Control is confirmed if the business owner establishes set hours of work. The independent contractor retains the right to establish his/her own hours of work.

8. Full-Time Work Is Required

An independent contractor is free to work when and for whom he chooses. If the worker is required to work a full-time schedule for the business owner, not on a project basis, this implies that the worker is restricted from doing other gainful work and has, therefore, surrendered some control and is more likely to be considered an employee.

9. Doing Work on the Employer's Premises

Control over the worker may be indicated if the work is performed on the premises of the business owner, especially if the work could be done elsewhere. While having an office off the premises indicates some freedom from control, this fact by itself does not mean that the worker is not an employee. If the business owner has the right to compel the worker to travel a designated route, to canvass a territory within a certain time, or to work at specific places, control is confirmed. An independent contractor typically can work either on or off the employer's premises.

10. Order or Sequence Set

Control is suggested if a worker must perform services in the order set by the business owner. Independent contractors retain the right to perform their services in any order and manner that gets the job done.

11. Oral or Written Reports

Requiring workers to submit regular oral or written reports to the business owner indicates control. Independent contractors have few obligations to submit reports or do so only as specified by contract.

12. Regular Payment by Hour, Week, Month

An employer-employee relationship is suggested when the worker is paid by the hour, week, or month and on a regular basis. Payment made by the job or on straight commission generally indicates that the worker is an independent contractor.

13. Payment of Business and/or Travel Expenses

If the business owner pays the worker's business and travel expenses, the worker is ordinarily an employee. Independent contractors pay their own expenses, except as specified within a contract.

14. Furnishing Tools and Materials

If the business owner furnishes tools, materials and other equipment, this implies an employer-employee relationship. Independent contractors furnish their own tools and equipment.

15. Significant Investment

If the worker has a significant investment in facilities and/or equipment s/he uses for performing services, this tends to indicate that the worker is an independent contractor. If the worker does not, that worker is more likely an employee.

16. Realization of Profit or Loss

If a worker can realize a profit or suffer a loss from services provided, s/he is generally an independent contractor. The worker who cannot is an employee.

17. Working for More Than One Firm at a Time

If a worker performs services for several unrelated persons or firms at the same time, that factor generally indicates that the worker is an independent contractor. Employees generally work on a non-project basis for only one business entity at a time.

18. Making Services Available to the General Public

Making services available to the general public on a regular and consistent basis indicates an independent contractor relationship. Not doing so indicates a level of control typically associated with an employee relationship.

19. Right to Discharge

The right to discharge a worker indicates that the worker is an employee and the person with this right is an employer. Independent contractors cannot be fired if they meet contract specifications.

20. Right to Terminate

If the worker has the right to end his or her relationship with the business owner at any time without incurring liability, that factor indicates an employer-employee relationship. Independent contractors are bound by the agreement to perform a service to completion or per contract.

For more information on this topic, please go to www.irs.gov.

Creating Your Own Corporation or Limited Liability Company

Many independent consultants create their own corporations or limited liability companies (LLCs) to get around the risk of being reclassified as employees. I have created my own LLC in Colorado, where I live. The laws regarding LLCs vary from state to state.

One way to create a limited liability company is to contact The Company Corporation at www.incorporate.com and do it yourself online. It costs about $600. Alternatively, you can hire an attorney to create your LLC. This will probably be more expensive. You can also follow the guidelines outlined in books that have been written to help small business people set up and manage LLCs. One such book is, *Your Limited Liability Company, an Operating Manual*, by Anthony Mancuso. This is a Nolo publication and comes with a CD-Rom containing the forms needed to operate your LLC. It costs about $50.

One of the biggest advantages of having a corporation or LLC is that the recruiting agency or consulting firm hiring you has a reduced risk of being considered your "employer" if you are already set up as an LLC. That means, among other things, that they have a reduced risk of being liable for employer payroll taxes for you if they are audited.

If you are one of five potential candidates an agency has for a contract opportunity, being set up as a corporation or LLC can increase your chances of being the one hired. Many recruiting agencies prefer hiring contractors who are already set up as a corporation or LLC. It makes you appear more professional and prepared than candidates that have not taken this step.

When you prepare invoices for your clients, you will use your corporate name. Your clients will then send you checks payable to your corporation. Therefore, you will need to open a corporate checking account.

Another advantage of incorporating is the limitation of liability. Although a corporation can be sued, the individual stockholders, employees, and officers are normally protected. However, if you are sued, the attorney for the plaintiff will probably name both the corporation and the officers as defendants in a lawsuit. Incorporating may not fully protect you as an individual. Of course, always consult with an attorney regarding limitations of liability with LLCs and corporations.

One of the biggest disadvantages of incorporating is the recordkeeping requirements. Periodic meetings may be required to maintain your corporation's status. You may also be required to file periodic statements with your state for payroll taxes, withholding, and identifying your servicing agent with the Secretary of State.

Taxation Options

There are multiple options when it comes to complying with government regulations regarding payroll taxes and self-employment taxes. The information here is being offered to you based on my own research as a lay person, not as a tax expert. You should always consult with a Certified

Public Accountant or tax attorney to determine the best method for your personal situation.

When you create a limited liability company, you can elect to be taxed personally for the profits coming from the LLC and report those earnings on Schedule C of your personal income tax return.

If you incorporate as an S corporation or create an LLC, have elected to be personally taxed for your organization's income, and report your earnings on Schedule C, then you will need to pay self-employment taxes on Schedule SE.

However, another option is to issue yourself payroll checks. If you choose to issue yourself payroll checks, then you would not report your income on Schedule C. Instead, your LLC would issue a W-2 earnings statement to you in January of the following year. You would then report your W-2 income on your personal income tax return, just as you would for any other W-2 statement issued by an employer.

When you issue yourself payroll checks, you are responsible for both the employer and employee portions of FICA taxes and Medicare. The recommended way to do this is to issue yourself payroll checks either quarterly or annually. Then you issue yourself a W-2 form at the end of the year. You also file a corporate income tax return, typically on IRS Form 1120S.

If you do elect to be taxed personally on the profits earned by your corporation or LLC, then you file a corporate income tax return every year. In this scenario, the corporation pays no income tax. You pay taxes on your profits as an employee of your corporation.

For more information on income taxes for the self-employed, see the chapter "Income Tax Considerations for the Self-Employed."

Always consult an attorney before choosing a business entity type or deciding to incorporate.

1099 vs. W-2

Many agencies and consulting firms will give contractors the option of being a "1099" contractor or a "W-2" hourly employee with no benefits. The term "1099" refers to the tax form that clients send to their contractors at the end of each calendar year.

Even if you are already incorporated, there may be compelling reasons to choose working as a W-2 hourly employee over working as a 1099 contractor. If you choose 1099, then you will submit periodic invoices with timesheets and expense reports and be paid as any other vendor would. Payment terms are typically fourteen to thirty days.

If you choose W-2, then you will be paid from the company's payroll system, typically once a week or every other week. You will not need to submit an invoice.

Here are some factors to consider when deciding which option to take:

- If you are a 1099 contractor, then you will be responsible for either: (1) all of your own employer and employee payroll taxes if you issue yourself payroll checks from your corporation or LLC, or; (2) self-employment taxes if you report your income on Schedule C of your personal income tax return.

- If you are an employee, you will only be responsible for the employee portion of payroll taxes, not the employer portion. Your client will deduct payroll taxes from your check.

- If you are an employee and are laid off due to lack of work, you should be eligible for unemployment benefits.

- If the firm you are working for goes out of business without paying you, employees have rights that are generally greater than 1099 contractors.

- If you are an older contractor and seeking to contribute large amounts of tax deferred earnings into a retirement plan, then 1099 might be a better way to go. (See the "Retirement Planning for the Self-Employed" chapter of this book for more details.)

- By choosing W-2, it is unlikely that you will have collection problems because you are an employee of the company, rather than a vendor.

- Hourly rates for W-2 employees are generally 10% to 15% lower than 1099 rates.

- Some agencies and consulting firms require proof of liability as well as errors and omissions insurance from their contractors. Some even require proof of workers compensation insurance. Employees are not required to have their own liability or workers compensation insurance.

- If you choose to go 1099, you can offset your taxable income with operating expenses such as supplies, advertising, and education in a way that will benefit you.

As you can see, there are many factors to consider.

All things being equal, you are typically better off being paid as a W-2 employee than as a 1099 contractor, as long as the rate is the same. This is because the company that hires you will pay the employer portion of payroll taxes instead of you. They will also pay you quicker and deduct withholding taxes for you. They might even deposit your net pay into your checking account. If your employer files bankruptcy, you will have a higher priority of getting paid as an employee than a contractor would.

If you are working under an LLC or an S corporation, here is one way you can comply with the federal payroll tax requirements. At the end of a calendar year, or quarterly during the year:

- Estimate your net profit for the year or quarter.

- Issue yourself a payroll check from your S corporation or LLC, deducting all required taxes.

- Remit the taxes, including withholding, to the government, through your bank.

- Issue yourself a W-2 statement at the end of the year.

- File payroll quarterly and annual tax returns with the government.

The other way would be to just report your earnings on Schedule C of your personal income tax return and pay self-employment taxes on Schedule SE. You may be required to make quarterly estimated payments to the government during the year if you choose this method.

Always consult with a Certified Public Accountant for income tax advice regarding these methods.

Contracts and Terms

Disclaimer: The author is not an attorney and does not dispense legal advice. The topics discussed in this section are from a layman's perspective only. Always consult your attorney if you have questions regarding legally binding contracts.

I use the standard ICCA consulting contract for my direct clients. When I am hired by consulting firms, they usually prefer to use their own contracts. There are many standard consulting contracts out there.

Here is a classic paragraph to watch out for when contracting with agencies and consulting firms:

Contractor agrees that Client controls the payment of fees to Contractor. Contractor shall only be entitled to payment from ABC Consulting after ABC Consulting has been paid by the Client, although ABC Consulting may, at its own discretion, pay Contractor prior to receiving payment from Client.

Never sign a contract if it contains a paragraph like this. While most agencies are ethical and pay their contractors on time, there are a few who use the excuse, "Our client hasn't paid us, so we can't afford to pay you." If you are offered a contract with a clause like this in it, just ask the consulting firm or agency to remove it or change it. Most will. If they won't, find another company to work for. Or ask them to hire you as a contract employee and put you on their payroll.

Also, beware of noncompete clauses. While most companies forbid you from soliciting their clients directly, which is customary, others will attempt to prevent you from working for any client in your field of expertise.

* * *

Owning a consulting business involves more than just writing code or configuring software. Setting up your business as a business is an important part of becoming independent. The type of business entity you create is dependent upon your needs and what you want to accomplish.

In my own experience, when I am called by recruiters, I am asked three questions:"What is your rate?" "Will you take less?" "Are you incorporated?" That third question has been validation that setting up my business as a limited liability company was a good decision.

Insurance for the Self-Employed

One of the byproducts of becoming an independent consultant is that you will probably become an expert in all kinds of insurance, whether or not you want to.

Shopping around for insurance is a time consuming consequence of becoming your own boss. In the past, when you worked as an employee for a company, you were most likely provided with company sponsored insurance programs such as health, dental, life, and disability. Because of their size, most employers are able to negotiate excellent group rates with insurance providers.

As the owner of a business, you will now be responsible for buying your own insurance.

I do not consider myself a genius in this area. But because I have spent so much time shopping for and learning about insurance, I will share with you what I have learned. For more accurate and current information on insurance, please contact an insurance company, agent, or broker.

Health Insurance

In my opinion, the best deal going for self-employed individuals is the Health Savings Account, or HSA. These are designed to work with "high deductible" insurance policies. Many health insurance companies have high deductible plans that work under the HSA guidelines.

Under an HSA, a self-employed individual buys a high deductible insurance policy. The deductible can be, for instance, $5000 a year for the whole family, or $2500 a year for each family member. Mine is $10,000 a year for the whole family. I bought the cheapest policy available ($300/month premiums). Generally speaking, the higher the deductible, the lower the premium.

For 2009, the IRS defines a high deductible policy as follows:

- An annual deductible of at least $1150 for an individual and $2300 for a family.

- Annual out-of-pocket expenses up to $5800 for individuals and $11,600 for families.

NOTE: Getting a private health insurance policy is not automatic. You have to apply. If you have pre-existing conditions or a history of cancer or heart disease, you might be rejected. This is unlike the group plans in which most employees are covered when they are hired.

If you are leaving an employer and cannot obtain private health insurance, another option is to take advantage of COBRA, which entitles you to keep your employer's coverage, but for a limited time and sometimes at a high price.

When you submit your medical bills, your insurance company will review the bill and determine the allowable fees. If the allowable fees are lower than the actual fees, most physicians will accept the lower amount. That saves you money.

Then you need to pay the provider. But if you have a Health Savings Account, instead of writing them a check from your personal checking account, you will have an account already set up at your HSA bank and will pay out of that. When you set up your Health Savings Account, you will also probably receive a debit card and can use it to make the payment.

For 2009, you can make tax deductible contributions to your HSA of $3000 for an individual and $5950 for family coverage. If you are fifty-five or over, there are provisions for "catching up" on your contributions. This means you can contribute more than what would otherwise be the maximum amount. For 2009, the catch up contribution for an individual is $1000 for that year and all years going forward.

Whether or not you have a Health Savings Account, as a self-employed person, your monthly insurance premiums are most likely deductible for federal income tax purposes. There are IRS requirements for this, such as having made a net profit for that tax year, so be sure to check IRS guidelines. The contributions to your HSA account are also deductible, again within IRS guidelines.

I recommend that you contact your insurance agent for more details on HSAs.

Here are just a few companies that offer health insurance for self-employed individuals and their families:

- Assurant—www.assurant.com

- Anthem—www.anthem.com

- Humana—www.humana.com

Liability Insurance

I have two liability insurance policies, one for general liability and one for errors and omissions (E&O). I purchased both policies from The Hartford.

I have had my general liability policy since 2001. My first direct client required it. The coverage is for $1,000,000 and the premiums are about $400 a year. Liability insurance will cover you in case you do damage to your client's property. You should carefully read your policy to see what is covered.

Errors and omissions insurance covers you in the event that you make a mistake while on the job that costs your client money. Your client can sue you for damages.

I purchased my first errors and omissions policy in 2007. The coverage is $500,000 and the premiums are about $1400/year. A consulting firm I worked for required it. More and more consulting firms and agencies are requiring their contractors to have errors and omissions insurance.

For details on what is covered by these policies, please contact your insurance agent or The Hartford. The Hartford is the only insurance company I know of that offers liability insurance to independent computer consultants.

Disability Insurance

If you are serious about being an independent contractor, then I would highly recommend buying a disability insurance policy. The best source of affordable disability insurance is professional trade associations. Private disability insurance can be very expensive.

The cost of this insurance varies. Here are some of the main factors that determine your premium:

- The amount of the monthly benefit you receive when you become disabled;
- The waiting period before the benefit payments start;
- The limit of the benefits (lifetime, dollar limit, or time limit); and
- Your age and occupation.

I have had a disability insurance policy for many years. I bought it through a trade association I belong to. The premiums are about $400 a year. The monthly benefit is $3000 for life with a sixty-day waiting period. It was the cheapest disability insurance I could find.

Companies that offer disability insurance include:

- The Guardian Life Insurance Company of America
- Ameriprise Financial

Life Insurance

I cannot begin to describe to you how many types of life insurance policies there are in the world. I have a term life insurance policy in the amount of $250,000. I pay about $400 a year.

The life insurance industry is extremely competitive, and I recommend that you shop around. Also, approval is not always automatic. You usually have to undergo some type of a physical exam.

I suggest that you consult with a life insurance expert before buying a life insurance policy.

Workers Compensation Insurance

Workers compensation insurance provides medical benefits and compensation for employees who are injured at work.

Requirements for this type of insurance vary from state to state. Check with your state's employment division to determine if you are required to buy workers compensation insurance.

* * *

When you step into the world of independent consulting, insurance is just one of the many business considerations you must explore. But it takes only one serious injury or one work related liability to remind you why you did your homework and got the insurance.

Of course, you hope to not need the life insurance for a long while and certainly not until you have had at least a few happy years in retirement. That means you also need to consider setting up a retirement plan.

Retirement Options for the Self-Employed

You will probably love your life and lifestyle as an independent computer consultant, but you will still probably want to retire one day. You may have fantasies of sitting on your front porch somewhere in the mountains, with a small trout-fed stream nearby. Or maybe you see yourself retiring to Mexico where you plan to sip margaritas and play golf on a regular basis. Even if you plan to stay in your current home and maintain most of your current activities when you retire, you will need money to support that lifestyle.

Once you become self-employed, you will no longer have an employer-sponsored retirement program, though you will be able to transfer your 401(k) if you have one. But the US government has provided many tax-deferred retirement options for the self-employed.

In my opinion, the best retirement option for self-employed individuals is the "individual 401(k)" or "solo 401(k)" plan. You can make tax deferred contributions to your plan as an employee *and* employer of your own corporation. You can also roll over your IRA and your employer-sponsored 401(k) into your own 401(k).

You can set up your own 401(k) at most banks and stock brokerage firms. Here are the highlights for individual 401(k) plans for 2008:

- The annual contribution into a solo 401(k) consists of two parts called a salary deferral and a profit sharing contribution.

Generally, both contributions are 100% tax deductible when made into a solo 401(k).

- Self-employed business owners may be able to contribute more into a solo 401(k) than a SEP-IRA or Keogh retirement plan at the same income level, therefore maximizing valuable tax deductible retirement plan contributions. This means a self-employed business owner can accumulate tax deferred retirement balances faster while reducing annual taxes at the same time.

- Self-employed business owners can contribute up to 100% of their first $15,500 of compensation in 2008 ($20,500 if age 50+). Compensation is defined as W-2 wages if incorporated or self-employment income if a sole proprietorship. This is the salary deferral contribution of the solo 401(k).

- The plan also lets business owners make tax deductible profit sharing contributions of up to 25% of compensation (wages), up to the annual maximum of $46,000 for the 2008 plan year. These profit sharing contributions are deductible on your corporate income tax return and therefore reduce payroll taxes. For sole proprietorships a 20% contribution can also be made into a solo 401(k).

- Note that the total of salary deferrals and profit sharing contributions cannot exceed $46,000 ($51,000 if age 50 or older) for 2008.

- Solo 401(k) plan contributions and investment earnings grow tax deferred. Withdrawals after age 59 1/2 are taxed as ordinary income. Withdrawals prior to age 59 1/2 may incur an IRS 10% premature withdrawal penalty as well as income taxes.

It is never too soon, and never too late to plan for retirement. I strongly recommend that you consider investigating the many retirement programs available to self-employed individuals. And because I am not an expert in retirement planning, do consult with a Certified Financial

Planner, Certified Public Accountant, or tax attorney before setting up a retirement plan.

Companies that offer individual 401(k) plans:

- Equity Trust—www.trustetc.com

- Bank of America

- Charles Schwab

- Dreyfus—www.dreyfus.com

- First Union Securities

* * *

Once you have thought through—and done something about—your retirement planning, your mind will be a bit more at ease when you contemplate all the advantages of retirement. Of course, the more money you have in your own pocket, the better you might find retirement. You also need to give consideration to the money you will pay the IRS as an independent computer consultant, with emphasis on being a good citizen *and* legally minimizing your taxes.

Income Tax Considerations for the Self-Employed

When you start your own consulting business and are being paid on a "1099" or contractor basis, you become responsible for the following taxes:

- Self-employment taxes if you are a sole proprietor (including LLCs electing taxation as sole proprietors).

- Payroll taxes if you are incorporated or an LLC (LLCs electing taxation as a corporation or partnership).

- State and federal income tax withholding and deposits.

Clients usually do not withhold taxes for you if you are an independent contractor.

The IRS requires that self-employed individuals either make quarterly estimated income tax payments to the government or issue themselves payroll checks on a quarterly basis. You should not wait until the end of the year to make your estimated income payments.

In 2008, the self-employment tax for individuals who are operating as sole proprietors is 15.3% of the first $102,000 of net profit reported on Schedule C of form 1040. On top of that, you will be responsible for federal and state income taxes.

Many self-employed individuals are shocked when they are completing their tax forms and discover that they owe thousands more than they expected. Self-employment taxes are sometimes unanticipated by independent consultants. See your CPA or tax attorney for more details.

Here is how it works for an incorporated individual (including those who have LLC designations as corporations or partnerships), as explained to me by my CPA. During the year, or at the end of the year, you issue yourself a pay check based on your corporation's profit. Most of your profit for the year needs to be paid out in the form of payroll checks, either quarterly or annually. There are payroll processing companies that will help you do this. Your corporation withholds money for employer payroll taxes, employee payroll taxes, and income taxes. These funds must be deposited by your corporation with a bank within a prescribed amount of time. Do not send federal withholding taxes directly to the IRS. You will be penalized if you do. They must be deposited with a bank.

So let's say that it's mid-December and your estimated profit for the year, after all of your business expenses, is $110,000. You could process a gross check for $100,000, minus deductions. You would need to deduct $6,200 for FICA (6.2% of the first $102,000 for 2008) and $1,450 for Medicare (1.45% of gross wages with no limit). In this example, you would have around $15,000 in federal withholding and $5,000 in state income tax withholding. Here is how this scenario would look:

Sample Year-End Payroll Calculation for an Incorporated, Self-Employed Individual for 2008, for Demonstration Purposes Only	$
Estimated Profit for the Year	110,000
Gross Payroll	**100,000**
Less:	
Employee FICA @ 6.2%	(6,200)
Employee Medicare @ 1.45%	(1,450)
Federal Income Tax Withholding (estimated)	(15,000)
State Income Tax Withholding (estimated)	(5,000)
Net Check	72,350
Subtotal amount owed to the government by 1/31/09 (Employee FICA + Medicare + Federal Withholding + State Withholding)	**27,650 (a)**
Add:	
Employer FICA @ 6.2%	6,200
Employer Medicare @ 1.45%	1,450
FUTA @ .62% of the first $7,000	43
State unemployment taxes (estimated)	300
Subtotal Employer Taxes (deductible on your corporation income tax return)	**7,993 (b)**
Total Owed to the Government by 1/31/09	**$ 35,643 (a+b)**

You would need to process your payroll check by December 31st. Then you would need to file federal and state payroll tax returns by January 31st and remit $35,643 to the government.

You will notice that there is a difference of $10,000 between the gross amount and the amount of business profit in this example. The reason for this is that you can deduct employer payroll taxes ($7993 in the above example) as a business expense on your corporate income tax return. You cannot deduct the employee portion. The difference between that $10,000 and the $7993 in employer taxes is $2007. This amount needs to be reported as "Other Income" on line 17 of your personal income tax return, IRS Form 1040. That way, all of your income is taxed, just the way the IRS likes it.

There is another item to be aware of. The amount of state income tax that you withhold during the year should be tax deductible on Schedule A of your federal personal income tax return, if you itemize deductions.

These government obligations often take the newly self-employed by surprise.

Deductible Business Expenses

You can reduce your taxable income by taking deductions for expenses related to your business. These include:

- Business related dues and subscriptions;
- Business related education and seminars;
- Supplies;
- Liability insurance;
- Postage;
- Advertising; and
- Contributions to a qualified retirement plan.

I have attended software conferences and taken classes and deducted the expenses from my consulting income for tax purposes. The conferences and classes must be business related to be deductible.

If you purchase equipment such as laptops and printers, you should be able to deduct the business portion of these on your income tax return. See your CPA for details.

This author does not claim to be an expert in the field of income taxes and, therefore, cannot render tax advice. You should always consult with a licensed Certified Public Accountant or income tax attorney if you have any questions about taxation.

* * *

As is often said, death and taxes are inevitable. But you can and should minimize the taxes you pay as an independent consultant. Learn the IRS guidelines for sole proprietors and/or small businesses. Employ a good CPA if you need to. This part of your business is too important to entrust to the advice of your next-door neighbor or your brother-in-law (unless they are CPAs).

Surviving Business Travel

Travel is inevitable for many independent computer consultants and it can be gruelling. Everything you can do to make travel easier will, ultimately, help your client as well as you because you will be in better shape to do the work for which you were hired. I have included some tips here to help you out. I have logged more than one million miles over the past few years and have learned a few things in the process. Here are a few insider tips on how to make business travel more tolerable.

Obtain Elite Status with Airlines and Hotels

One of the most important things you can do for yourself to survive business travel is to obtain elite status with as many airlines as possible. With elite status, you can have the following benefits:

- Free upgrades to first class;
- Higher priority for standby flights;
- Priority seating;
- Early boarding; and
- Bonus miles.

What I discovered a few years ago was this: If you have elite status with any airline, you can obtain elite status with most other airlines, even if you have never flown on them before. And it doesn't cost a dime!

Here's How it Works

If you fly—a lot—you can earn elite status on most major airlines based on the number of miles you travel on their airline in any given calendar year.

One of the biggest advantages to having elite status is being moved up on the standby list. Once, when my wife and I were returning home from a vacation in Boston, our flight to Denver on United was cancelled. There were only five seats available on the next (and last) flight to Denver that night. Because I had Premier Executive status with United, we were able to get on that last flight. Many people ended up spending the night in Boston . . . but we were not among them.

Examples of Elite Status Programs

Every major airline has its own rules and benefits for its elite members. For example, United Airlines has three levels of elite status based on the number of miles you fly in a calendar year:

- Premier: 25,000 miles gets you 25% bonus miles and the opportunity for free upgrades to First Class, as well as higher priority for getting on standby.

- Premier Executive: 50,000 miles gets you even higher standby priority plus double miles.

- 1K: 100,000 miles gets you all of the above (including double miles) with more free upgrades and an even higher priority for standby.

American Airlines has a similar system with silver, gold, and platinum status.

How to Obtain Elite Status Without Ever Flying on that Airline

If you can obtain elite status with just one airline, you can usually get other airlines to match it.

In 2004, I was offered a consulting contract with a company in Dallas. Dallas is a major hub for American Airlines. I live in Denver, where United is the major carrier. When I looked at the flight schedules, I discovered that American had the best times and fares.

At the time, I had Premier Executive status with United (50,000 miles a year). I called American and asked if they would match my United status. I told them that if they would grant me Gold status, I would fly them to Dallas instead of United.

They told me to fax them a copy of my United statement showing all of the trips I had flown on United over the past year. On the fax cover sheet, I indicated that I was starting a long-term project in Dallas and described my situation. I also included my American Airlines AAdvantage number. A couple of weeks later, I received my "courtesy" Gold status card with American.

A similar thing happened with Air Tran. In 2006, I was offered a long-term project in Atlanta. I checked the flight schedules and Air Tran had the best fares and flight times to Atlanta from Denver. Air Tran is Atlanta-based.

I had never flown on Air Tran. I called and asked them if they would give me elite status. The first person I spoke with said, "No!"

I called again a couple of days later and talked to a different person. She said, "We normally don't do that, but you can fax your United statement to us and we'll think about it."

A week later I received my Air Tran elite status card.

Before you ask for elite status, you must enroll in that airline's frequent flier program. When you fax in your request, be sure to have your frequent flyer number on the cover sheet. Even if you have never flown on that airline, you can still enroll in their frequent flyer program.

I Have Done This with Many Airlines

Over the past few years, I have had also obtained "courtesy" elite status with Delta, Northwest, Frontier, and Continental. Once, at the Atlanta airport, my United flight home was delayed for several hours. I walked over to Delta and they flew me home in First Class.

Recap

Here is a recap of how to obtain elite status with most major airlines:

- Have legitimate, earned status on at least one major airline.

- Have a legitimate, compelling reason to obtain status on a competitor's airline.

- Enroll in the competitor's frequent flyer program.

- Fax the competitor your frequent flyer statement showing trips taken over the previous year and write your frequent flyer number for the competitor's airline on the cover sheet.

- Do not take "No" for an answer! I was turned down by Air Tran and Delta and kept trying until I succeeded.

- Most airlines will only give you elite status for one year. After that, you must earn it. And you can only obtain "courtesy" elite status once per lifetime per airline. If you start out with Gold status, some airlines will downgrade you to Silver after the first year. That is what American and Delta did with me. After your Silver status expires, then your elite status with that airline expires for good.

Hotels

You can also obtain elite status with major hotel chains. The levels of status for Marriott are:

- Silver: 10 nights in a calendar year.

- Gold: 50 nights in a calendar year.

- Platinum: 75 nights in a calendar year.

Once you achieve status with Marriott, it's good through the next calendar year.

You can receive bonus points and room upgrades based on your status level. Some hotels even have courtesy snacks and free bottled water for those who have status. Hotel points can be used for free stays. I frequently use these points.

You will have to earn these levels every year. If you don't, the chain will usually bump you down one level in the following year. I know that Hilton sometimes has promotions for those who lose their status. If you stay at their properties for a certain number of nights in a specific time frame, they will bump your status back up.

The nice thing about having Platinum and Diamond VIP status is that Marriott and Hilton will both guarantee you a room at any of their participating hotels, even if they are sold out, as long as you book forty-eight hours in advance. To be on the safe side, though, it is best to book your room seventy-two hours in advance. On one occasion I called Hilton on a Friday afternoon to book a room for Sunday night. They claimed that I had not called far enough in advance.

For Hilton, elite status works like this:

- Blue: less than 10 nights or 4 stays in any 12-month period.
- Silver:10 nights or 4 stays in any 12-month period.
- Gold: 36 nights or 16 stays in any 12-month period.
- Diamond VIP: 60 nights or 28 stays in any 12-month period.

I once checked into a Hilton Hotel in California and room service brought complimentary milk and cookies to my room.

I have not tried to obtain elite status with competing hotels by offering to stay at their properties and sending them Marriott or Hilton statements. Try it. See if it works for you.

Travel Services

There are services you can purchase to make your business trips a lot more survivable. These include joining airline lounge clubs and buying a Clear card.

Airline Lounge Clubs

Many airlines have lounge clubs you can join. These lounges typically have free beverages, snacks, and newspapers. Most of these lounges offer business services as well, such as conference rooms, fax machines, and printers. An example is United's Red Carpet Club, which maintains lounges at airports around the world. The cost to join United's Red Carpet Club is around $500/year. I deduct this fee on my income tax return as a business expense. You can also use frequent flyer miles to join the Red Carpet Club.

Other major airlines have their own lounge clubs. Continental Airlines has the Presidents Club, and Delta Airlines has the Crown Room.

Clear Card

Another service you can buy is the Clear card. Having a Clear card enables you to bypass the long security lines at many airports in the United States.

After undergoing a thorough background check, including finger printing and eye scans, you will receive your own Clear card. Once you have a Clear card, going through security is like having a valet service when you park your car. Their agents help carry your personal belongings as they move you up to the front of the security line. The cost is around $200/year, which I deduct as a business expense. For more information about this program, go to www.flyclear.com.

Working from Home

What is the best way to survive business travel? Work from home! I work from home whenever possible. Some clients are fine with this; some are not. One arrangement that has worked for me is to work thirty-six hours a week on-site, and the other four hours at home on Fridays.

If you travel to a client site, you need to bill forty hours a week, every week, to make your trips worthwhile. In my early days, I sometimes billed thirty-four or thirty-seven hours a week. On days when I was not busy, I left work early and went back to the hotel.

I no longer do that. I can always find work to do that will benefit my client. Rather than work shorter hours, I periodically take a week off, or work from home for a week.

Take a Break!

I have gone for many stretches of twelve, fifteen, and even nineteen weeks in a row on the road. I no longer do that. I made a great deal of money during those stretches and when I saw those checks, it motivated me to work as many hours as I could.

The problem I had—and this is true for most travelling consultants—was extreme burnout. After doing twelve or fifteen weeks in a row on the road, I began to question my reasons for living. I became depressed. The money didn't mean much to me because I was always away from home and exhausted.

As a general rule, I do not work more than four weeks in a row on the road. Even if it means making less money, I am fine with that. I have found that most of my clients are very understanding when it comes to taking time off, or occasionally working from home.

Experience the Locale

When I travel on business, I try to experience the local sights, cuisine, and culture. Even in a small town such as Beloit, Wisconsin, I was able to attend a Snappers minor league baseball game. At that game, I watched a young Prince Fielder and a young Tony Gwynn Jr. take the field. They became star players with the Milwaukee Brewers.

I love baseball and whenever I am on the road, I try to attend a local baseball game. Over the years, I have seen the New Jersey Jackals, the Fort Worth Cats, the Appleton Timber Rattlers, the Buffalo Bisons, and the Fort Myers Miracle.

I have been to about half of all the major league ballparks, including those in Boston, Seattle, Detroit, Atlanta, Oakland, Cleveland, and Kansas City.

I frequently work in New York City. While there, I have seen many Broadway musicals and plays. I have also seen Rush in concert at Radio City Music Hall. I have flown my wife out to join me a couple of times for weekend activities and it was fabulous for both of us! And New York restaurants are great.

My clients gladly paid for my hotel rooms and rental cars on the weekends I stayed in town. My not flying home saved them hundreds of dollars in airfare. It also saved wear and tear on me. I used my frequent flyer miles to fly my wife out in First Class.

In 2006, I worked on a project in Fort Lauderdale, Florida. Fort Lauderdale is a beautiful resort town, just a few miles north of Miami. I flew my wife, son, and even my mom out to join me. We stayed at a great hotel, right on the beach.

And once, when working in Charleston, South Carolina, the company put me up at a bed and breakfast inn downtown. Charleston is a beautiful, historic, seaside city and was wonderful!

* * *

Business travel is a necessity for me and it is tough. If you travel extensively as an independent computer consultant, make life easier for yourself by gaining elite status on airlines and at hotels, by building in downtime, and by treating yourself to a little luxury now and again. It will make your business travel more tolerable—which means your client will have a better worker and your family will have a happier independent consultant when you do get home.

Dealing with Difficult Clients

If there is one thing that differentiates this book from all other books on consulting, it is that I will tell you, in detail, just how difficult some clients can be.

Don't get me wrong. Most of my clients have been wonderful. For the most part, they have been cooperative, appreciative, understanding, flexible, and sociable. I have made many lasting friendships and business relationships. These good clients make up about 85% of all of my clients.

Unfortunately, there is the other 15%. For whatever reasons, these clients are hostile, uncooperative, inflexible, accusatory, confrontational, and outright mean. They hate consultants and their people hate each other. They go out of their way to make life as difficult as possible for consultants. They will sabotage consultants' work, find fault where there is none, and blame the consultants for every possible thing they can think of.

I have a few theories as to why some clients are so awful. Here are a few:

1. Consultants usually make more money than their clients. Most of the people with whom I work realize that consultants make pretty good money and, perhaps, there is some resentment because of it. I have read many Internet blogs in which this situation is discussed.

2. Some employees are defensive and protective about their jobs. Many companies who hire consultants do so because they have tried and failed to accomplish tasks with their own personnel. These companies often hire consultants as a last resort and when they do hire them, the reception is often less than warm.

3. Some corporate cultures foster environments of mistrust, envy, secrecy, paranoia, and hostility. Some employees hate each other just as much as they hate consultants.

4. Some companies are completely dysfunctional. They are unorganized and lack direction. Their employees resist change, regardless of the benefits change can bring. Incompetence runs up and down the organization chart.

5. Some people are just mean by nature and have miserable personal lives. They bring their personal problems to work and try to impose their misery on others.

I do not have quick solutions for dealing with difficult, dysfunctional clients. But I will share a few war stories that might be helpful. In all of the stories that follow, the names of the companies (consulting and client companies), the company staff with whom I dealt, and some locations have been changed.

The Client from Hell

By far the worst client I ever had was Ayniss Enterprises, a small company in Oklahoma I worked for in 2004. I had just come from a long-term project where the people were friendly, sociable, and appreciative. I guess I just assumed that all clients were that way.

I knew I was in trouble as soon as I arrived on my first day. The client had assured me that their software would be installed and configured before I arrived. My job as a financial modeling consultant is to build models, not install software. When I got there, I found that the box containing the software CDs had not even been opened. It went downhill from there.

I put together a ten-week project plan. By the second week, the project was already behind schedule. As I attempted to organize the team and come up with some sort of plan, the individuals with whom I was assigned to work became increasingly hostile and difficult. The lead team member, Justine, was not simply unhelpful as I attempted to resolve problems with the group; she was the most hostile person with whom I had to work.

By the third week, the insults, accusations, and threats became intolerable. I called the person who hired me, Jenny, the chief financial officer, and set up a meeting. When I set up the meeting, I told her I wanted to give her an update on the team's progress. I brought Justine with me to the meeting. Prior to the meeting, I had not told Justine much about what I planned to discuss with Jenny.

At the meeting, I very calmly made it clear to Jenny that I would no longer tolerate Justine's accusations, insults, and threats. I told Jenny, with Justine sitting right next to me, that the project was behind schedule and at risk of failing. I also said that I would gladly resign if the company was dissatisfied with my work, allowing them to find a replacement with whom they might be happier.

Justine was furious. Justine told Jenny that I was incompetent and difficult to work with.

Jenny's response was, "Mitch is in charge and you need to listen to him."

Things did not improve after the meeting. Instead, they got worse. Justine refused to talk to me, as did the other team members. The project got further behind schedule, and was hopelessly out of control.

The beginning of the end came during week five. Without notifying me in advance, Jenny brought in another consultant to review my work. The following Monday, the IT director, Randy, called me into his office. He asked me how things were going and I replied, "Badly."

Randy said, "Son, I think you need to find yourself another gig. I'm giving you your two weeks notice."

My reply was, "Two weeks notice? Are you kidding me? I can be out of here in fifteen minutes!"

He urged me to stay the two weeks. I told him I would finish out that week but would not commit to the following week.

I left his office and pulled Justine into a conference room. I politely told her, "I've just been given my two weeks notice by Randy. I want you to know that if you are unhappy with my work, I can leave today. You don't need to give me any notice at all."

Justine's response shocked me.

"I need your knowledge. I want you to stay at least until the end of this week," she said.

She hadn't spoken to me for days before this.

On Thursday afternoon, Randy approached me and said, "It's up to you. You can come back next week if you want."

"It's not up to me, it's up to you," I said. "I haven't accomplished a thing all week. If you want me to come back next week, I will."

I did not return the following week. I have had no contact with Ayniss Enterprises since and have no idea if their project was successful.

As an independent consultant, you should never tolerate clients who are hostile and confrontational. When things begin to get bad, do try to resolve the problems with the work team. But if that fails to improve the situation, do not hesitate to go up the chain of command to the next level of management. I have done this in a few situations. It may cost you your job, but there are always other jobs. Fight the good fight and take a stand. Remember, the main two reasons companies hire consultants are experience and leadership. Let them experience your leadership! Your self-dignity and self-worth are more important than money.

It was during my stay in Oklahoma that I learned my wife was pregnant with my son, Joshua. Two weeks after I left Oklahoma, my wife and I went on a fabulous seven-day cruise to Alaska. We ate like pigs and had a wonderful time. When I returned home, I was offered a project with a liquor distributor. It was one of the best projects I have ever been on. When I left, they gave me several bottles of high-priced booze as a gift.

Joshua Paioff was born on January 7, 2005.

George Herbert, an English cleric and metaphysical poet, once said "Living well is the best revenge." I agree.

Ethics Anyone?

The most unethical organization I have ever worked for was a large government agency called the State of Confusion.

I was hired by SOC right after Joshua was born. I signed an employment contract with them that committed me to them full-time for a period of five months. The hourly rate was $165. I had other prospects who were interested in hiring me at the time, but after I signed the contract with SOC, I told them I was unavailable. I had never worked for a government agency before and assumed that they intended to honor the terms and conditions of their own contract.

SOC was completely unprepared for me when I arrived. They had no place for me to sit and there was no agenda. I spent the first week moving around from conference room to conference room and accomplished absolutely nothing.

As I was preparing to leave for the airport that Friday, Mary, the person who had hired me, approached me and said, "We have decided to keep you on the bench next week." I asked her what she meant and she responded, "Don't come in next week."

I said, "Then you still want me to come in the following week, right?"

"Yes," she replied.

I didn't argue with her about going for a week without pay ($6600).

I called Mary the following Thursday to confirm that I was to return the next week. I had already bought a plane ticket and made hotel reservations.

Mary said, "We have found someone internally at SOC to do the work we hired you to do. We don't need you anymore."

Surprised, I pressed the point. "You have someone in your organization who has experience building complex financial models using business intelligence software?"

"Yes," she replied.

I knew she was lying.

I'm not sure what happened at SOC. I submitted my timesheet for forty hours for the week that I was "on the bench." Since my contract with SOC precluded me from accepting full-time employment with other companies, I knew that I was legally entitled to be compensated for that second week. I showed my contract to a couple of employment attorneys and they agreed with me that I was entitled to compensation.

SOC refused to pay me for the second week. I sent demand letters to their executive director and was denied compensation. I thought about suing them, but even though I had a solid case, I decided it was not worth the effort. I was at least eventually paid for the first week.

The Client from Hell and Back

Just when you think you have seen it all, a client can come along who is so mean and vindictive that they will go out of their way to harm your career.

Recently, I was hired by a large company in the Memphis area, Evil Industries. I had brief telephone interviews with two of their people before I went to Memphis. One was Jack, an IT specialist. The other was his boss, Peter. It was supposed to be a six-week project. I was assigned to work with Jack.

Jack was abrupt and unfriendly over the telephone. Peter was businesslike and respectful. Peter told me I was being brought in to do some "documentation." Neither of them mentioned anything about problems at their company. They just asked me a few standard questions about my background.

Jack was rude, impersonal, and hostile from the very beginning. He told me that he would soon be leaving for a two-week vacation and that the only reason I was there was to fill in for him while he was gone. None of this had been discussed during my two telephone interviews.

Peter had failed to disclose that Jack was very angry about having a consultant come in. Jack was very protective and secretive about the work he was doing. No one could figure out what Jack did and Jack was not about to let anyone in on his territory.

I started out documenting their system. Jack sat about ten feet away from me. Every time I asked Jack a question, he said, "I'm too busy to talk to you. Just email the question to me." Sometimes when I approached him, his response was an angry, "Now what!"

By the third day, the situation was already intolerable. Jack had terrible communication skills. Though I attempted to do what I thought he had asked me to do, everything I showed him was met with criticism and fault finding. Then he began making accusations of incompetence. I was unwilling to tolerate that.

I reported my issues to the consulting firm that sent me to Evil Industries, a firm called ABCO. They were very understanding and contacted Peter. ABCO and I tried everything we could think of to mitigate the situation.

I also went directly to Peter several times to complain about Jack. The first few times I asked to meet with him, he said he was too busy to talk to me. He finally set aside five minutes for me. I shut the door to his office and told him I was receiving constant negative feedback from Jack, as well as accusations of incompetence. I said that I would not tolerate the insults and told him that if the company was dissatisfied with my work, they should hire someone else.

The situation deteriorated from there. Jack's insults and accusations became worse. I continued to complain to Peter and ABCO on an almost daily basis.

By the third week, I decided enough was enough. I was not going to tolerate the verbal abuse and hostility any longer. I was determined to avoid a confrontation, but it came anyway. On Thursday, as I was getting ready to leave for the airport, I asked Jack to sign my timesheet. The arrangement I had with ABCO was that the client needed to sign my timesheet for me to get paid.

Jack refused to sign my timesheet.

"Is there a problem with my timesheet?" I asked.

He said, "No. I'm too busy to sign it."

I decided right then and there that if someone didn't sign my timesheet before I left for the airport, I was not returning.

I called Peter on his cell phone. I told him what had happened and explained that someone needed to sign my timesheet immediately. He said that he was in a meeting and would have to talk to Jack before he made a decision.

I waited an hour, until around 4:15 p.m. I had to leave by 4:30 to catch my flight. Evil Industries had an instant messaging system. I sent Peter an IM. *I need to leave for the airport soon. I must have my timesheet approved before I leave. I just want you to understand that if my timesheet is not approved before I leave, I will not be returning here next week. I have notified ABCO of this situation, and we hope that you will resolve it quickly.*

Peter's response came back a few seconds later. *Drop off your badge at the guard's desk on your way out.* That was followed by *I will contact our legal department to see if we have to pay you.*

A day earlier, Peter had asked me to stay an additional three weeks because he was so pleased with my work. He had also described to me, in great detail, his loathing for Jack. He had said that Jack was an arrogant, argumentative, antisocial individual who was despised by just about everyone he worked with. Peter had reported that Jack was unable to function as a team member and often had heated confrontations with his coworkers that were overheard by others.

Peter said that Jack had been put in charge of a computer project there a few months earlier. But because of Jack's poor communication skills, no one at Evil Industries could understand what he was doing, nor could they monitor his progress. The project had gotten so far behind schedule, several people at Evil Industries had needed to work late nights and weekends.

Peter also told me that Jack had gone on a one-week vacation a few months earlier. Jack had assured Peter that Evil Industries' budgeting and forecasting system would run "just fine" in his absence. While Jack was out of town, the entire budgeting and forecasting system crashed. No one could reach Jack. And no one at Evil Industries knew how it worked or how to fix it. Keep in mind that Evil Industries is a huge multinational conglomerate.

Peter explained that one of the reasons I was hired was to figure out what Jack did. Peter wanted me to document the system and monitor it while Jack was gone. Of course, none of this had been disclosed to me during my telephone interviews with them.

So I turned in my badge and left. The following week, by pure coincidence, I was hired by another division of Evil Industries in Oregon for what should have been a six-month project. Somehow Peter found out that the Oregon division had hired me and, apparently, told the project manager there some terrible things about me.

Then the Oregon people fired me. That firing permanently damaged the relationship I had with the consulting firm that sent me to Oregon, BIPCO.

The consulting firm that had sent me to Evil Industries' Memphis office (ABCO) was very supportive and paid all of my invoices. They told me that I handled the situation well, and apologized on behalf of their client. They also said that they would no longer do business with Evil Industries. I keep in contact with the people at ABCO on a regular basis.

I left both divisions of Evil Industries with my dignity and self-respect intact. I have no regrets about my actions. If I am ever in circumstances like that again, I will conduct myself in the exact same manner.

I ran into Jack a few months later at a conference. I didn't talk to him. I looked up his profile and discovered that he was still employed at Evil Industries. That gave me a lot of satisfaction, knowing that his boss, Peter, and the others at Evil Industries who were so hostile to me were still having to tolerate his behavior.

Guaranteed to Fail

I will finish off the stories in this chapter with one that demonstrates how consultants are sometimes put into situations with no possible chance of success.

A few years ago, I was hired by InDenial Company, a consulting firm in Charlotte. They asked me to build financial forecasting models for their client, NoClue, in rural Georgia.

The first order of business for me was to have a discussion with InDenial's salesperson, Donald. I later discovered that Donald was just about to leave InDenial Company. I guess he was just trying to close one last deal before he left.

In a call to NoClue, he had told them that his company could implement a complete budgeting and forecasting system for them in twelve consulting days. In reality, these projects typically take fifty to sixty consulting days to complete.

I reviewed the statement of work that InDenial Company had prepared. The proposed twelve days included three days of classroom training, along with the implementation. I called Donald and politely explained to him that no consultant could possibly implement this system in twelve days. He said that his client understood this and that NoClue would do most of the work themselves.

Then we arranged for a conference call with Benny, the NoClue IT director. Benny became quite agitated when I explained to him that I could start the implementation and do the training in the twelve days, but would not be able to complete the project in that time frame. He stated that Donald had told him that the whole thing could be done in twelve days. I assured him it would take much longer.

Benny then called Carl, the vice president of InDenial Company, to complain about me. Donald also complained to Carl about me. Then Carl called me. Carl accused me of not being a team player and told me I needed to "come on board." I told Carl that I would do the project for them, but that NoClue would ultimately be disappointed because their expectations were unrealistic. He was in complete denial, and told me to, "Just do what we tell you to do."

The project began with me doing classroom training at InDenial's headquarters in Charlotte. Since NoClue did not have a classroom facility at their location, they needed to come to us. They agreed to do that, but refused to pay for my travel expenses from Denver to Charlotte. It is customary in the consulting industry that clients pay for consultants' travel expenses. When Benny was asked why he would not pay for my travel expenses, his response was, "We have to drive all the way to Charlotte. Why should we pay for Mitch's expenses too?"

The classroom training went well. That consumed three of the twelve consulting days. The next step was for me to go to NoClue's office in extreme rural Georgia. When I say "extreme rural," I mean *really* extreme. The town had a post office and a church. No gas station, no McDonald's, not even a liquor store. The nearest hotel was thirty miles away. The nearest eating establishment was about fifteen miles away.

To say that the folks at NoClue were unsophisticated would be a major understatement. They had been completely duped by Donald. When I arrived on Monday morning, the first thing I discovered was that one of their IT people, Kramer, had decided to reconfigure the entire system that had been installed by an InDenial technician the previous week. That reconfiguration caused the whole system to crash. I spent the first two days there on the phone with the technician, trying to get the system back up and running. By Tuesday afternoon we were finally able to get one workstation running. (I later learned that the same InDenial technician had to go back out there a second time to do a complete reinstall.)

Then I started the requirements gathering phase. When I asked the company's finance people how they wanted to do their budgets, they looked at me with blank stares. I asked them the standard questions: "Do you budget sales at the product level?" "Do you budget payroll by named employee?" "Do you want a separate budget by location?" They had no clue. As it turns out, they had never budgeted anything there. They assumed that I was going to magically build them a sophisticated budgeting model without any input from them.

This story has a very unhappy ending. After that first week, NoClue called Carl, the vice president at InDenial Company, and complained about me. They said that I asked too many questions and reported that they had received no value for the five days I was there. They demanded that InDenial Company send out another consultant. I was fired from the project.

A few weeks later, I received an email from Carl. The email stated: *As has been previously discussed with you, NoClue has refused to pay us for the full forty hours that you worked at their location. Your check will reflect the 50% reduction.* I was furious. This had never been discussed with me. I called Carl to protest. I never would have agreed to a reduced amount. Carl refused to pay me the full forty hours. That permanently ended my relationship with InDenial Company.

I later learned that NoClue had initially refused to pay InDenial for *any* of the time I spent there. InDenial Company negotiated a compromise with them, without involving me, and then InDenial penalized me for doing "a bad job."

That is the only time in my seven years of being an independent consultant that I was not paid for work I did. Sometimes the stars are aligned for you . . . and sometimes against you.

Carl left InDenial Company shortly thereafter. Donald, the salesperson, was already gone before I even went to Georgia.

I ran into Benny, the IT director, at a conference a couple of years later. He was still working for NoClue. I asked how the financial modeling implementation had fared. He said, "Oh, we never finished it."

I asked him why.

He stated, "Our chief financial officer left the company."

I said, "Why should that make a difference? There were several people there involved with the project."

He replied, "It just didn't happen."

How to Handle Problem Situations

If leadership is one of the things clients look for in consultants, then great communication and great interpersonal problem solving skills are two critical components of leadership. Independent computer consultants must have more than technical skills. They must also have good communication skills and must be able to skillfully navigate troublesome on-site situations.

Can you completely avoid problem situations? Not in my experience. As mentioned earlier, 85% of clients are wonderful and the other 15% are . . . well . . . less than wonderful. With that great 85%, you will need solid communication skills and the ability to effectively solve interpersonal problems. With the other 15%, you will need those skills—in spades—and you may still have a less than satisfactory outcome.

Here are a few things I have learned over the years about communication and interpersonal problem solving:

- Be polite and respectful. You learned these skills in elementary school and they are as useful in adulthood as they were then. Model these two things and you improve your chances of being treated politely and with respect.

- Communicate, communicate, communicate. Never assume that what has not been said is implicitly understood. Be clear.

- If you experience a problem, do not ignore it, expecting or hoping that it will go away. It will probably not go away. It will probably get worse if you do not address it.

- If the problem is with a person, address it with that person first, if at all possible. Be clear and specific. Remember to be respectful, regardless of how frustrated you may be. Among other things, that means avoiding eye rolling, finger pointing, and other negative body language. That also means avoiding sarcasm, questions to which you already know the answers, and other verbal sparring that will put the other person on the defensive. Stop talking once you have said what needs to be said. When you shut up, you create a vacuum that only the person to whom you are speaking can fill.

- There are natural consequences to every problem. With computer consulting projects, the natural consequences often include missed deadlines, an implementation that cannot be completed, and cost overruns. Respectfully point out the natural consequences that will occur if you do not come to resolution as one method for gaining cooperation from others during problem solving.

- If your attempts fail, do not hesitate to go up the chain of command. Use the same direct, respectful approach when you escalate the issue.

- Express appreciation when problems are solved. If they cannot be solved and you leave the assignment, avoid taking verbal potshots on the way out. Your reputation as a respectful, reasonable person is worth preserving.

Sometimes nothing you can do will salvage the situation. Do your best . . . and be willing to walk away, if necessary. Know that you are not alone if you have had clients from hell. And remember that the 85% of clients who are great more than make up for the handful that are not.

Common Mistakes and How to Avoid Them

When I first started out as an independent consultant, I tried to learn as much as I could about the industry. I approached other independent computer consultants for advice, but none were willing to give it. I also read several books about starting a consulting business. Many of these books were excellent, but still lacked some of the practical nuts and bolts help I needed.

I ended up making many serious, costly mistakes. In this chapter, I will describe the mistakes I made in detail. In doing so, I hope to help you avoid at least some of the ones I made.

The Biggest Mistake Made by Newly Independent Consultants

By far the biggest and costliest mistake I have made (and I have made this mistake several times) is accepting an all-inclusive rate. What is an all-inclusive rate? Let's say you quote a project at $100/hr. plus travel expenses and the client's response is that they need a quote with an all-inclusive rate. That is their way of saying, "We would prefer that you stay at Motel 6, eat all your meals at Burger King, rent a Ford Focus, and fly on Cheap Seats Airlines."

My first long-term project as an independent contractor was for a company in Chicago. I quoted them $75/hr. plus expenses. They came back to me and said, "We need an all-inclusive rate." I did some quick math in my head and responded with $105/hr. They accepted the quote. I figured that the $30/hr. difference ($1200/week) would just about cover all of my expenses.

What I had not considered was that it was spring and the airfares from Denver to Chicago were about to go up from $500 to $800. Also, the hotels in suburban Chicago are very expensive, around $150 to $200 per night.

I ended up spending the next six months sleeping in cheap hotels, renting subcompact cars, and eating fast food. It wasn't my client's fault, it was mine. I did a lousy job of negotiating. They probably would have accepted $115/hr. as an all-inclusive rate if I had proposed it. I will never know for sure. As it turned out, I never once cleared the $75/hr. that I originally quoted. It was more like $68/hr.

I might have learned, but I did a bad job negotiating all-inclusive rate contracts on two more projects after that.

Here are some other reasons why you should never accept an all-inclusive rate:

- If you work a short week, say, 32 hours, you still have to buy a plane ticket to get there and back. Your net effective rate will be even lower because the cost of airfare will be spread out over fewer billable hours.

- You deserve to stay in decent hotels and eat decent food. You are a professional and should live like one.

- If you occasionally work from home, how are you supposed to determine your hourly rate?

Here is how I now handle these situations. First, I quote a ridiculously high all-inclusive rate, like $180/hr. (or $2400/week) for travel expenses, based on an hourly consulting rate of $120. Clients almost never accept these markups, although *one* of my clients actually did.

Another approach is to propose spending limits in your hourly-plus-expenses contract, such as, "Airfare not to exceed $900 per trip" and "Hotel not to exceed $190 per night." Some clients like this approach.

Contract Clauses to Watch Out For

Some agencies and consulting firms will throw in a clause in the "Compensation" section of the contract that reads something like this:

> *Contractor agrees that Client controls the payment of fees to Contractor. Contractor shall only be entitled to payment from ABC Consulting after ABC Consulting has been paid by the Client, although ABC Consulting may, at its own discretion, pay Contractor prior to receiving payment from Client.*

Never, ever sign a contract that contains this provision. If the client ends up not paying the agency—for any reason—you will have absolutely no recourse against either the agency or their client. The statement, " . . . Client controls the payment of fees to Contractor" is completely false. The agency or consulting firm controls the payment of your invoices.

Whenever I see this clause in a contract, I politely refuse to sign it until the clause is either removed or reworded. For me, this has never been a deal killer. The firms I work with always comply with my request in one way or another. Remember: *Everything* is negotiable. That holds true no matter how big or small the firm you are subcontracting with is.

Not Working from Home

This was another dumb one for me. It took me a few years to realize that most clients will let you work from home. Not every week or all the time, but occasionally. Now I work from home whenever I can.

Accepting a Low Rate on a Long-term Contract and Hoping for a Raise

This is a bad strategy. The likelihood that you, as a contractor, will ever get a raise is extremely remote. I know of only one person who has been successful at this. If you need the income, and there is only the one gig available, you might have to take the low rate. But the rate of pay you negotiate going in will probably be what you will receive for the project's duration.

I fell prey to this. A few years ago, I accepted a low rate on an assignment and hoped I could get a raise once the project was up and running. I had been out of work for a few weeks and needed the income. The assignment ended up lasting for eight months. I asked for a raise on three different occasions and was turned down every time.

Accepting a Salaried Job when You Suspect It Is a Short-Term Project

This topic is covered in the "How to Market Yourself Effectively" chapter.

Tolerating Abusive, Hostile, and Confrontational Clients

This topic is discussed at great length in the "Dealing with Difficult Clients" chapter.

* * *

These are just a few of the many mistakes I have made as an independent consultant. I mention them here so you can avoid them. Can you avoid mistakes completely? Of course not. It would be impossible for me to detail every kind of mistake you can make as you gain experience. Experience is a good teacher. My hope is to save you some grief, speed up the learning process, and help you avoid some costly mistakes. The rest is up to you.

CHAPTER 13

Preparing Yourself for Self-Employment

There is no such thing as the perfect time or scenario to become self-employed. Motivated individuals will seek out opportunities and take action when the timing is good, but not necessarily perfect.

Once you go out on your own and experience the freedom, self-empowerment, and prestige of being an entrepreneur, you will wonder why you waited so long to make the leap. But make no mistake about it. Becoming self-employed isn't a piece of cake. It involves hard work, creative thinking, and a high tolerance for risk. Not everyone succeeds. But if you do succeed, and I hope you do, the rewards can be tremendous.

Here are a few things to think about before you take that giant leap:

- Look for long-term contract opportunities that will allow you to resign from your current position and go right into consulting.

- Curtail your spending on big-ticket items. Delay purchases of homes, cars, and luxury goods.

- When you start your first project, begin working on your own website.

- Research health insurance options before you quit your job.

- Try to leave your employer on good terms. You might need them as a reference. They might also be a potential client!

- Consider setting up a corporation or limited liability company.

- Consider acquiring liability insurance, disability, life, and errors and omissions insurance.

- Have an emergency fund set aside in case your project ends and you are out of work for a time.

- Network with as many consultants in your field as possible. Begin *before* your first project ends. Call them on the weekends to see how they are doing. Offer to help them with technical issues. Referrals are the best source of new clients. You will get better projects at higher rates from referrals than anywhere else.

Here is another option: If you have recently been laid off, consider taking on a short-term contract position. It might turn into a long-term contract.

Visualize Success

I have found that visualizing the end result of my dreams helps me to achieve goals. Before I ever became an independent consultant, I visualized myself walking into a client's building, attending meetings, talking with important people, and showing them how to implement systems. I imagined what my business cards would look like. I visualized what it would feel like to tell people that I was self-employed. I also imagined buying a new car and going on vacations with the money I earned.

Once I had that vision, I took the necessary steps to achieve that goal. I talked to other independent consultants. I read books and took classes. It ended up taking me many years to achieve that goal . . . and it was well worth it.

Act Today!

There may never be a perfect time to become an independent consultant. Consider the following quotes:

> *"Take time to deliberate; but when the time for action arrives, stop thinking and go in."*
>
> —*Napoleon Bonaparte*

> *"Never take career advice from someone who makes less money than you."*
>
> —*Mitch Paioff*

Thank you for reading this book. I wish you the best of luck.

Appendix

Sample Consulting Contract

INDEPENDENT COMPUTER CONSULTANTS ASSOCIATION

STANDARD FORM CONSULTING CONTRACT

THIS AGREEMENT is made as of _____,
20_____between _____ ("Client") and
_____
_____("Consultant").

WITNESSETH, THAT:

WHEREAS, Client desires to retain the services of Consultant, and Consultant desires to provide such services; and

WHEREAS, the parties desire to enter into a Consulting Contract setting forth the terms and conditions of their agreement and their understandings.

NOW, THEREFORE, in consideration of the premises and the mutual covenants, promises, and agreements herein contained and for other good and valuable considerations, the receipt and sufficiency of which are hereby acknowledged, the parties, intending to be legally bound hereby, agree as follows:

   1. **Services.** Consultant agrees to perform for Client the services listed in the Scope of Services as set forth on Exhibit A attached hereto and incorporated herein by reference (the "Services"). Consultant shall have access to Client's staff and resources as deemed necessary by Consultant, in Consultant's sole and absolute discretion, to perform the Services provided for by this Agreement.

2. Rate of Payment for Services. Client agrees to pay Consultant for Services in accordance with the schedule contained in Exhibit B attached hereto and incorporated herein by reference and executed by both Client and Consultant.

3. Invoicing. Consultant shall invoice Client, at Client's address as set forth in Section 15 hereof, for the Services rendered, and Client shall pay the amount set forth on such invoices to Consultant, at Consultant's address as set forth in Section 15 hereof, within ten (10) days of receipt thereof.

4. Confidential Information. (a) In the course of performing the Services referenced herein, Consultant and Client may come into possession of the other parties' financial and/or other business information pertaining to such other parties' business which is not published or readily available to the public, including, but not limited to, trade secrets, research, development, marketing concepts and plans, training, pricing information, sales techniques, lists of customers and vendors and other information pertaining to the business conducted by either Consultant or Client which is received from the agents or employees of either party ("Confidential Information"). Confidential Information shall not include information which is generally known or easily ascertainable by third parties of ordinary skill and competence in computer system design and programming, nor shall it include information already known to the receiving party or disclosed to the receiving party by a third party without violation of a duty of confidentiality to the disclosing party.

(b)   Consultant and Client each acknowledge and agree that Confidential Information is important to, and greatly affects the success of, both parties in a competitive marketplace. Consultant and Client agree that during the course of their relationship and at all times thereafter, Consultant and Client shall hold in the strictest confidence, and shall not use for either parties' personal benefit, or disclose, duplicate or communicate to or use for the direct or indirect benefit of any other person, firm, corporation or entity, any Confidential Information without the prior written consent of the other party, or unless Consultant is required to do so in order to perform the Services, or pursuant to a court order or by operation of law.

5.   **Staff.**   Consultant is an independent contractor and neither Consultant nor Consultant's staff is or shall be deemed to be employed by Client.   Client is hereby contracting with Consultant for the Services described on Exhibit A and Consultant reserves the right to determine the method, manner and mean by which the Services will be performed. Consultant is not required to perform the Services during a fixed hourly or daily time and if the Services are performed at the Client's premises, then Consultants time spent at the premises is to be at the discretion of the Consultant; subject to the Client's normal business hours and security requirements. Consultant hereby confirms to Client that Client will not be required to furnish or provide any training to Consultant to enable Consultant to perform Services required hereunder. The Services shall be performed by Consultant or Consultant's staff, and Client shall not be required to hire, supervise or pay any assistants to help Consultant perform the Services under this Agreement.   Consultant shall not be required to devote Consultant's full time nor the full time of Consultant's staff to the performance of the services required hereunder, and it is acknowledged that Consultant has other clients and Consultant offers services to the general public. The order or sequence in which the work is to be performed shall be under the control of Consultant. Except to the extent that the Consultant's work must be performed on or with Client's computers or Client's existing software, all materials used in providing the Services shall be provided by Consultant. Consultant's Services hereunder cannot be terminated or cancelled short of completion of the Services agreed upon except for Consultant's failure to perform the Agreement's specification as required hereunder and conversely, subject to Client's obligation to make full and timely payment(s) for Consultant's Services as set forth in Exhibit B, Consultant shall be obligated to complete the Services agreed upon and shall be liable for non performance of the Services to the extent and as provided in Paragraph 10 hereof. Client shall not provide any insurance coverage of any kind for Consultant or Consultant's staff, and Client will not withhold any amount that would normally be withheld from an employee's pay. Consultant shall take

appropriate measures to insure that Consultant's staff is competent and that they do not breach Section 4 hereof.

Each of the parties hereto agrees that while Consultant is performing Services under this Agreement and for a period of six (6) months following the performance of such Services or the termination of this Agreement, whichever is later, neither party will, except with the other party's written approval, solicit or offer employment as an employee, consultant, independent contractor, or in any other capacity to the other party's employees or staff engaged in any efforts under this Agreement.

6. Use of Work Product. Except as specifically set forth in writing and signed by both Client and Consultant, Consultant shall have all copyright and patent rights with respect to all materials developed in the course of performing the Services under this Agreement, and Client is hereby granted a nonexclusive license to use and employ such materials within the Client's business.

7. Client Representative. The following individual _____ shall represent the Client during the performance of this Agreement with respect to the Services and deliverables as defined herein and has authority to execute written modifications or additions to this Agreement as defined in Section 14.

8. Disputes. Any disputes that arise between the parties with respect to the performance of this contract shall be submitted to binding arbitration by the American Arbitration Association, to be determined and resolved by said Association under its rules and procedures in effect at the time of submission and the parties hereby agree to share equally in the costs of said arbitration.

The final arbitration decision shall be enforceable through the courts of the state of Consultant's address [15(ii)] or any other state in which the Client resides or may be located. In the event that this arbitration provision is held unenforceable by any court of competent jurisdiction, then this contract shall be as binding and enforceable as if this section 8 were not a part hereof.

9. **Taxes.** Any and all taxes, except income taxes, imposed or assessed by reason of this Agreement or its performance, including but not limited to sales or use taxes, shall be paid by the Client.

LIMITED WARRANTY

10. **LIABILITY.** CONSULTANT WARRANTS TO CLIENT THAT THE MATERIAL, ANALYSIS, DATA PROGRAMS AND SERVICES TO BE DELIVERED OR RENDERED HEREUNDER, WILL BE OF THE KIND AND QUALITY DESIGNATED AND WILL BE PERFORMED BY QUALIFIED PERSONNEL. SPECIAL REQUIREMENTS FOR FORMAT OR STANDARDS TO BE FOLLOWED SHALL BE ATTACHED AS AN ADDITIONAL EXHIBIT AND EXECUTED BY BOTH CLIENT AND CONSULTANT. CONSULTANT MAKES NO OTHER WARRANTIES, WHETHER WRITTEN, ORAL OR IMPLIED, INCLUDING WITHOUT LIMITATION, WARRANTY OF FITNESS FOR A PARTICULAR PURPOSE OR MERCHANTABILITY. IN NO EVENT SHALL CONSULTANT BE LIABLE FOR SPECIAL OR CONSEQUENTIAL DAMAGES, INCLUDING, BUT NOT LIMITED TO, LOSS OF PROFITS, REVENUE, DATA, OR USE BY CLIENT OR ANY THIRD PARTY, REGARDLESS OF WHETHER A CLAIM OR ACTION IS ASSERTED IN CONTRACT OR TORT, WHETHER OR NOT THE POSSIBILITY OF SUCH DAMAGES HAS BEEN DISCLOSED TO CONSULTANT IN ADVANCE OR COULD HAVE BEEN REASONABLY FORESEEN BY CONSULTANT, AND IN THE EVENT THIS LIMITATION OF DAMAGES IS HELD UNENFORCEABLE THEN THE PARTIES AGREE THAT BY REASON OF THE DIFFICULTY IN FORESEEING POSSIBLE DAMAGES ALL LIABILITY TO CLIENT SHALL BE LIMITED TO ONE HUNDRED DOLLARS ($100.00) AS LIQUIDATED DAMAGES AND NOT AS A PENALTY.

11. **Complete Agreement.** This agreement contains the entire Agreement between the parties hereto with respect to the matters covered herein. No other agreements, representations, warranties or other matters, oral or written, purportedly agreed to or represented by or on behalf of Consultant by any of its employees or agents, or contained in any sales materials or brochures, shall be deemed to bind the parties hereto with

respect to the subject matter hereof. Client acknowledges that it is entering into this Agreement solely on the basis of the representations contained herein. In the event of a conflict in the provisions of any attachments hereto and the provisions set forth in this Agreement, the provisions of such attachments shall govern.

12. Applicable Law. Consultant shall comply with all applicable laws in performing Services but shall be held harmless for violation of any governmental procurement regulation to which it may be subject but to which reference is not made in Exhibit A. This Agreement shall be construed in accordance with the laws of the State indicated by the Consultant's address [15(ii)].

13. Scope of Agreement. If the scope of any of the provisions of the Agreement is too broad in any respect whatsoever to permit enforcement to its full extent, then such provisions shall be enforced to the maximum extent permitted by law, and the parties hereto consent and agree that such scope may be judicially modified accordingly and that the whole of such provisions of this Agreement shall not thereby fail, but that the scope of such provisions shall be curtailed only to the extent necessary to conform to law.

14. Additional Work. After receipt of an order which adds to the Services initially provided for as set forth in Exhibit A of this Agreement, Consultant may, at its discretion, take reasonable action and expend reasonable amounts of time and money based on such order. In the event Consultant provides such additional services requested by Client, Client agrees to pay Consultant for such action and expenditure as set forth in Exhibit B of this Agreement for payments related to Services.

15. Notices. All notices, requests, demands and other communications hereunder shall be in writing and shall be deemed to have been duly given when personally delivered or two (2) business days after deposited with the United States Postal Service, certified or registered mail, postage prepaid, return receipt requested, addressed as follows (or to such other address as either party may designate by notice given in accordance with the provisions of this Section):

(i) Notices to Client should be sent to:

(ii) Notices to Consultant should be sent to:

16. Assignment. This Agreement may not be assigned by either party without the prior written consent of the other party. Except for the prohibition on assignment contained in the preceding sentence, this Agreement shall be binding upon and inure to the benefits of the heirs, successors and assigns of the parties hereto.

IN WITNESS WHEREOF, the parties hereto have signed this Agreement as of the date first above written. **THIS CONTRACT CONTAINS A BINDING ARBITRATION PROVISION WHICH MAY BE ENFORCED BY THE PARTIES.**

Client _____

Type Name and Title _____

Consultant _____

(This is a Standard Form Contract which may or may not require revision by the individual consultant's legal counsel. It is recommended that each consultant review the legal requirements pertaining to the consultant's State of operation with counsel licensed to practice in that State. Various States have laws that require that disclaimers of liability or arbitration provisions must be printed in enlarged print or that specific language be used, which may or may not be contained in this form. This should be reviewed with the counsel in the State in which each Consultant operates.)

For use by ICCA Members only.
Copyright© 1996
Independent Computer Consultants Association.

Independent Computer Consultants Association
11131 South Towne Sq., Suite F
St. Louis, MO 63123
Phone 314-892-1675
(Revised 1/97)

Reprinted with permission from the Independent Computer Consultants Association.

Index